EX
LIBRIS

Gabriel N Cherish

The World Cup
A Very Peculiar History™

With NO added time

'Some people believe football is a matter of life and death. I can assure you it's much, much more important than that.'

Bill Shankly, former Liverpool FC manager.

For my son, Jack – a fellow
Spurs and Lewes FC supporter

DA

Editor: Jamie Pitman
Editorial Assistant: Rob Walker

This revised edition published in Great Britain in MMXIV by
Book House, an imprint of
The Salariya Book Company Ltd
25 Marlborough Place, Brighton BN1 1UB
www.salariya.com
www.book-house.co.uk

HB ISBN-13: 978-1-909645-21-9

WARNING: The Salariya Book Company accepts
no responsibility for the foul tackles in this book.
They are included only for their historical interest
and may not be suitable for modern use.

1 3 5 7 9 8 6 4 2
A CIP catalogue record for this book is available
from the British Library.
Printed and bound in China.
Printed on paper from sustainable sources.

The
World Cup
A Very
Peculiar
History™

With NO added time

Written by
David Arscott

Created and designed by
David Salariya

Illustrated by
Mark Bergin

BOOK HOUSE
a SALARIYA imprint

'If there is one thing on this planet that has the power to bind people it is soccer.'

Nelson Mandela

'Everything I know about morality and the obligations of men, I owe it to football.'

Albert Camus

'If hosting it keeps some of our politicians on the straight and narrow for a few years it will have been worth the effort.'

South African journalist David Bullard before the 2010 World Cup

'Brazil goes into every World Cup expecting to win, so when it is in Brazil it is expected even more. You can't understand what the World Cup means to our country.'

Ronaldinho before the 2014 World Cup

'The World Cup needs a brilliant Brazilian team.'

Football pundit Alan Hansen

Contents

STATS CARD

Countries making most appearances in World Cup finals* before 2014:

Brazil	20
Germany (FRG/Germany)	17
Italy	17
Argentina	15
Mexico	14

Most consecutive wins in finals matches before 2014:

11	Brazil	2002–2006
7	Italy	1934–1938
6	England	1966–1970
6	Brazil	1970
6	Brazil	1978–1982
5	Uruguay	1930–1950
5	Uruguay	1950–1954
5	Germany FR	1954–1958
5	Brazil	1958–1962
5	Brazil	1962–1966
5	Poland	1974
5	Argentina	1986
5	Italy	1990
5	France	1986–1998

* Throughout this book 'finals' refers to the tournament itself (and 'finalists' to the teams who have come through the qualifying rounds to take part in it), while 'Final' refers to the deciding match at the end of the tournament – between the two 'Finalists'.

HOW IT ALL KICKED OFF

As this book is being written by an Englishman it naturally begins with the fact that it was our fellow countrymen who gave this best of all possible sports to the world, with the Football Association being founded as early as 1863.

Unfortunately it must then promptly admit what readers of other nationalities won't be slow to point out – that it wasn't very long before the rest of the world not only caught up with us, but was controlling, dribbling and passing the ball rather better than we were.

It's particularly galling to acknowledge that the story of the World Cup itself begins not with the English but with their traditional enemy across the water.

Yes, it was the French who in 1904 were chiefly responsible for founding FIFA, or the Fédération Internationale de Football Association. (The name's a bit of a give-away, isn't it?)

By now the game was catching on all over the globe, and the French idea was to get the British to share their expertise with other countries so that they could form a world governing body for the sport. Sad to say, the Brits weren't interested!

The awkward squad

First of all, in May 1902, the secretary of the Dutch football association wrote to the FA in London, and it took two months for him to get a non-committal reply. Then the FA suggested the idea be put on hold until their next meeting – in June 1903. What was the hurry?

Young Johnny Bull
refused to play with the
other boys.

It was the dogged young French journalist Robert Guérin who got things going. His first idea was for a football federation of European nations, and he twice visited London in the hope of persuading the FA to play ball.

He bent the ear of the FA secretary Frederick Wall and its president Lord Kinnaird, but he received the snooty response that they 'couldn't see the advantage' of his proposal. A writer for *Le Matin*, Guérin had an apt phrase to sum up his dealings with the arrogant English.

FIFA presidents

1. Robert Guérin (France) 1904–1906
2. Daniel Burley Woolfall (England) 1906–1918
3. Jules Rimet (France) 1921–1954
4. Rodolphe Seeldrayers (Belgium) 1954–1955
5. Arthur Drewry (England) 1955–1961
6. Stanley Rous (England) 1961–1974
7. João Havelange (Brazil) 1974–1998
8. Sepp Blatter (Switzerland) 1998–present

His talks, he said, had been 'like slicing water with a knife'.

In the end Guérin decided to go it alone. He called a meeting in Paris, and FIFA was established by representatives from France, Belgium, Denmark, Holland, Spain, Sweden and Switzerland. Germany were on stand-by.

With the 28-year-old Guérin installed as its first president, FIFA immediately drew up a list of rules, one of which firmly put the English in their place: 'The International Federation is the only organisation with the right to organise an international competition.'

From this moment on, FIFA would rule the world game.

Olympic muscle

Football was at last recognised as an Olympic sport in 1908. England won both that first tournament (in London) and the following one (in Stockholm) in 1912, but power was shifting: the FA had run the London event, but it was FIFA who took over in Stockholm.

An *ill-fated* cup

The first World Cup trophy was sculpted by Abel Lafleur in gold-plated sterling silver and lapis lazuli. Later named after FIFA president Jules Rimet, it was in the form of an octagonal cup held by Nike, the Greek goddess of victory. Unfortunately it suffered several indignities:

When the Second World War broke out in 1939 it was in the possession of Dr Ottorino Barassis, the Italian vice-president of FIFA, because Italy were then the holders. He hid it in a shoebox under his bed throughout the war.

In 1966 it was stolen while on display at an exhibition in London ahead of the World Cup final there. It was eventually discovered under a hedge in south-east London by a mongrel dog called Pickles.

Brazil won the trophy outright in 1970 by becoming champions for the third time. In 1983 it was stolen again – from the headquarters of the Brazilian Football Association – and it hasn't been seen since.

Its successor is a solid gold trophy simply called the World Cup. It's lent to the winners for four years, but remains the property of FIFA.

The Jules Rimet Trophy

The English did soon join FIFA, and were to provide three of its presidents, but they developed a habit of pulling out of it for one reason or another – for years on end.

Certainly the French influence on early world football was far more substantial:

- **Robert Guérin was FIFA's first president.**
- **Jules Rimet, the longest serving FIFA president, launched the World Cup .**
- **Abel Lafleur sculpted the first trophy.**
- **France played in the first World Cup match.**

Whistle in the windpipe

Another Frenchman who played a leading role in the development of international football was Henri Delaunay.

He sat on the first FIFA board, was a prime mover in instigating the World Cup and as early as the 1920s was promoting the idea of a European Champions Cup.

Delaunay had become a referee after his playing career was over, but he retired following a nasty accident. When the ball struck him full in the face two of his teeth were broken and he swallowed his whistle.

13

1914–1918

If, as legend has it, English and German soldiers played a scratch game of football together during the famous 1914 Christmas truce in no-man's land between the trenches, this was the only 'international match' for many years.

Once the carnage of the First World War was over, England and its allies resigned from FIFA because they felt obliged to draw up a long 'no-go area' of banned opponents – not only those with whom they'd been at war but any other nation which had agreed to share a pitch with their former enemies.

Shamateurism

The Olympic games eventually got going again in 1924, with FIFA running the football tournament. England had just rejoined the organisation, but along with the other British football associations and Denmark it declined to take part in the contest (in Paris) because it wasn't happy about what the organisers meant by the word 'amateur'.

This is when the lovely word 'shamateurism', ('sham amateurism') was born. Nobody was supposed to be paid for taking part in the Olympics, but wasn't it reasonable for the athletes to be paid out-of-pocket expenses?

The cash provided him with the protection he needed in this unstable economy.

Not as far as the British were concerned. They were horrified when, ahead of the 1928 Amsterdam Olympics, FIFA decided that amateurs should be allowed 'broken time' payments to compensate for their loss of earnings and to cover other costs.

And who would decide how much to pay them? Ah, that would be a matter for the individual football associations – so perhaps it wasn't surprising that the British should smell a rat. The system was wide open to abuse.

Goodbye - again!

What did they do about it? Well, of course they resigned from FIFA again, and this time they wouldn't return to the fold until after the Second World War was over, in 1946.

Mind you, FIFA and the FA continued to talk to one another. William Pickford, a committee member of both, put the FA's case very simply: 'We have nothing against FIFA, but our people here prefer to manage their own affairs in their own way, and not be entangled in too many regulations.' *Plus ça change!*

Pity the poor ref!

William Pickford was one of football's pioneers who helped devise its early rules. Chairman and president of the English FA from 1937 to 1938, he wrote thousands of newspaper articles about the game, and in 1906 he published a book called *How to Referee*.

It wasn't aimed only at the refs, though. Pickford hoped it would 'instil a better grasp of essential points in the minds of a class singularly ill-informed upon them – the players.'

Here are a few of his essential tips for referees:

- Don't forget that players are not machines, but are human and possess a keen sense of injustice.
- Don't let criticism hurt you: some people rejoice to see a referee writhe under it. It tickles them, and really if you are a good referee it cannot harm you.
- Don't be afraid, but be bold and fear not.
- Don't worry your head about the noise spectators kick up. Free Britons have queer ways of enjoying themselves.
- Don't go on refereeing if your eyesight gets bad, or you get old and slow.

The Olympic football tournament went ahead very happily without the absentees. South American football was now thriving, so it wasn't a shock when Uruguay won the 1924 tournament (beating Switzerland in the Final) and repeated the achievement four years later (overcoming Argentina in a replay).

But it was time to create a genuine world championship, and Jules Rimet realised that by disengaging it from the Olympics, FIFA could make it an unashamedly professional event open to all players. Problem solved!

The deal was done at FIFA's 1928 congress in Amsterdam, when an organising committee was formed: the very first World Cup was to be held in 1930.

Money

Football is a delightful game, exciting to play and to watch, but the story that now begins to unfold is not for the pure-hearted. FIFA had created a monstrous juggernaut – a large and colourful contraption that it would desperately seek to control as it careered around the globe attracting an endless and ever-growing procession of devotees, hangers-on and downright crooks. It would become big business, the greatest sporting show on earth. Nearly everyone (politicians, businessmen, betting syndicates, strutting players, humble fans) would want something from it.

And money spoke right from the beginning. At its 1929 congress FIFA decided that it would take ten per cent of the gross income for itself. Although that left what might seem a generous ninety per cent for the host nation, there was an obvious catch: the hosts would have to take all the risks, spending vast amounts of money on stadiums and other facilities and hoping they would get their money back. Who was up for it?

Five European countries which had originally declared an interest in holding the tournament (Holland, Hungary, Italy, Spain and Sweden) immediately took a step back. This was the year of the Wall Street Crash, don't forget, signalling the start of the Great Depression. Money was getting harder to come by.

That left only one contender: Uruguay, the reigning Olympic champions, whose government was prepared not only to finance the entire cost of the tournament, but offered to pay the travel and accommodation costs of all the other teams involved. FIFA simply couldn't say no.

We are sailing

But how many other countries would be bothered to turn up? Uruguay was a long way from Europe – all of three weeks by steamer back in 1930.

Two months before the inaugural World Cup was to kick off not one European team had signed up for it. The British were outside FIFA, and there were refusals from Austria, Czechoslovakia, Germany, Hungary and Switzerland, plus the four European countries who had at first shown an interest in staging it but had balked at the cost.

Even France wavered (it would have been truly disastrous if Jules Rimet's own country had pulled the plug on the competition), and the Latin American football federations threatened to resign from FIFA because of what they regarded as a gross insult. (Some of them would boycott the next two World Cups in Europe in retaliation.)

Just in time a compromise was cobbled together, and four very average European teams agreed to take part: France, Belgium, Romania and Yugoslavia.

The French squad left for the three-week crossing on 18 June, picking up the Romanian and Belgian squads early on and the Brazilian team when their boat called in at Rio de Janeiro. Yugoslavia travelled under their own steam, arriving at Montevideo in Uruguay four days after the others, on 8 July.

And so the very first World Cup could at last get under way – but how fitting that it should do so in a spirit of unseemly back-biting, financial wrangling and national pride . . .

1930

- **Host country:** Uruguay.

- **Finalists:** Argentina, Belgium, Bolivia, Brazil, Chile, France, Mexico, Paraguay, Peru, Romania, Uruguay, USA, Yugoslavia.

FACT FILE

- **What happened:** With only 13 countries taking part, several of them simply making up the numbers, the tournament was organised into four groups – one of four and three of three.

  France v Mexico and USA v Belgium, which kicked off at the same time, were the first World Cup matches ever played.

  In the Final, Uruguay, the Olympic champions and the favourites, beat Argentina 4–2 in front of a crowd of 93,000, after being 2–1 down at the interval.

- **Champions:** Uruguay.

- **What happened next:** The Argentina striker Guillermo Stábile's international playing career spanned only the four matches he played in this first World Cup (he scored in every one of them), but he later became manager of his national team and was in charge of Sweden in 1954.

CHAPTER ONE

POLITICAL FOOTBALL

You may well ask why a small country like Uruguay, which had a population of only two million at the time, should take the very great risk of staging such a potentially ruinous spectacle as the first World Cup.

Cynics usually tell us to 'follow the money' when answering such questions, but this time it was a matter of following the prestige.

Uruguay did, as it happens, come out of the tournament with a profit, but what mattered above all else was the glory.

It was exactly a hundred years since the country had won its independence from Spain, and what better way of celebrating this proud centenary than an event which would capture the attention of the entire world?

Uruguay was no banana republic and certainly did have something to shout about. It had a booming economy based on livestock, and its people enjoyed votes for all, an official eight-hour working day and unemployment benefits. It could afford its generous offer to finance the other twelve competing teams.

It never rains ...

Somehow, though, it also had to fulfil a promise made to FIFA that a huge new stadium would be built in Montevideo – developed from scratch in eight months, three of them falling in the 'rainy' season (which meant a season of steamy downpours).

They just made it. Some early matches had to be played at the club grounds of Peñarol and Nacional, but the (almost completed) Centenario Stadium was ready for the Final.

A few oddities

They did things differently in 1930. For example:

- The Uruguay forward Héctor Castro, who scored in the Final, had only one hand. He was a carpenter, and he'd lost the other one to an electric saw.

- When Bolivia came out for their first game each player had a large letter on his shirt. They lined up to spell out the words 'Viva Uruguay' in honour of the host nation.

- In the Brazil v Bolivia match three players on each side wore berets, while in the Cup Final itself the referee, the Belgian John Langenus, was dressed in his usual cap and plus-fours.

- Manuel Ferreira, the captain of Argentina, was missing from their second game because he'd popped back to Buenos Aires to take a law exam.

- During their match against Argentina, the American trainer Jack Coll had to be helped off the pitch in a daze. Some said he'd dropped a bottle of choloroform, while the US team manager said he'd been temporarily blinded by smelling salts.

- In the Final two different balls were used as neither team could agree on who should provide the ball. In the end Argentina supplied the ball for the first half, Uruguay the second.

A 64-year goal famine

Bolivia played just two matches in the first World Cup finals, losing to Yugoslavia and Brazil and by 4–0 both times – though they did have four 'goals' disallowed in their first game. Their fans would have to wait patiently until 1994 for another chance to score, because that's when they next appeared in the finals. They lost their first game 1–0 to Germany, drew 0–0 with South Korea and then at last struck gold by netting against Spain. (They lost 3–1.) Hats off to Erwin Sánchez – although his shot took a huge deflection on the way.

José tells his grandchildren about the disallowed goals he saw in Montevideo

And what happened when Uruguay won the trophy? The players were not only feted as national heroes, but they were all rewarded with a plot of land and a new house. It obviously mattered very much indeed!

A football-mad monarch

Someone else looking for some scattered stardust was King Carol II of Romania. We won't go into his tangled love life, but suffice it to say that after some juicy scandals he renounced the throne in 1925, only to return home and reclaim it the very month before the FIFA finals kicked off.

What's all this got to do with the World Cup? Well, the German-speaking Carol wasn't highly regarded by his subjects, but now he saw a chance of improving his reputation and indulging himself at the same time. He was simply nuts about football.

He asked the employers of Romania's players to grant each one a full three months' leave on full pay, and when they arrived in Uruguay he was there to select the team. Hoorah!

No (since you kindly ask), this story doesn't have a happy ending. Romania did beat Peru 3–1 in a game remembered only for attracting the smallest crowd in World Cup finals history (officially just over 2,500, but in reality around 300) and for the first ever sending off – a man named Plácido! They then crashed 4–0 to the hosts and were on their way home.

STATS CARD

As this was the inaugural World Cup, it inevitably threw up a long list of 'firsts':

- First World Cup goal – Lucien Laurent in France's 4–1 defeat of Mexico.
- First penalty – Carlos Vidal for Chile against France. (He missed it.)
- First player sent off – Peru captain Mario de Las Casas against Romania.
- First own goal – Manuel Rosas for Mexico against Chile.
- First set of brothers to play in the finals – Rafael and Garza Gutiérrez of Mexico.
- First set of brothers in a World Cup Final – Juan and Marino Evaristo of Argentina.
- First hat-trick – Guillermo Stábile for Argentina against Mexico.

Carol survived as king for another ten years, after which he was forced into exile, but Argentina's defeat in the Final had an immediate effect in Buenos Aires. Within days President Hipólito Irigoyen had been overthrown in a coup – the desolation and fury of the fans adding a little extra fuel to the revolutionary flames.

Enter the fascists

If the Uruguayan government's big spending and King Carol's tinkering with Romania's team selection were harmless examples of political interference, much more sinister forces would be at work during the next two World Cup finals.

What would FIFA do about Italy's request to stage the 1934 tournament? A reminder, should your history be shaky, that the Fascist dictator Benito Mussolini had been in power for ten years, had outlawed all political parties but his own and was imprisoning, torturing and killing his political opponents.

His admirers, on the other hand, liked the way he kept crime – other than his own – under control, kept employment high and spent money on things like impressive new buildings and public transport. As they said, he 'got the trains running on time'.

FIFA discussed Italy's application no fewer than eight times, which shows that at least some of its committee members were aware of the signal they'd be sending out if they caved in. But of course they *did* cave in – and if that surprises you, then you haven't picked up the early hints in this book that FIFA has always been as eager to seize its opportunities as have the rapacious politicians who've coat-tailed the World Cup at every turn.

One of Italy's attractions was that it already had some high-quality stadiums, with sport and fitness at the forefront of the Fascist agenda. It was also wealthy enough to finance the tournament, paying the other competing countries in the national currency, lire, rather than in pounds or dollars. This, claimed the newspaper *La Nazione*, was 'official recognition' that people had more confidence in the lire than other currencies. Pure spin!

1934

FACT FILE

- **Host country:** Italy.

- **Finalists:** Argentina, Austria, Belgium, Brazil, Czechoslovakia, Egypt, France, Germany, Holland, Hungary, Italy, Romania, Spain, Sweden, Switzerland, USA.

- **What happened:** The cup holders, Uruguay, dropped out, angered by the lukewarm European response to their own tournament four years earlier.

  The competition was organised on a knock-out basis from the beginning, so that Argentina and Brazil (both beaten in the first round despite being seeded) had travelled some 8,000 miles for a single game.

  Italy, the favourites, beat the USA 7-1, Spain 1-0 (after a replay) and the fancied Austrians 1-0 before coming from behind to beat Czechoslovakia 2-1 in the Final.

- **Champions:** Italy.

- **What happened next:** Italy announced that they'd made a profit of a million lire from the finals.

What the world now had to put up with was a stream of heavy propaganda aimed at proving how wonderful the nationalist regime was.

Jules Rimet complained that Mussolini was acting as though he were the FIFA president, but there was not a fat lot he could do about it. In fact the dictator (the self-styled 'Il Duce', or leader) not only interfered with the running of the tournament but provided his own trophy, the Coppa del Duce, which was about four times bigger than FIFA's.

Straight-arms and swastikas

Come Italy's first match of the tournament in the Stadio Nazionale del Partito Nazionale Fascista in Rome, there sat the jowly leader in a jaunty yachting cap, smiling broadly while the Italian team, the referee and the linesmen gave straight-arm fascist salutes. Up in Florence meanwhile, the German team trotted out with a swastika on their flag. Another dictator had recently taken over there – Adolf Hitler, who was about to launch his own brand of horrors on the waiting world.

'My cup's bigger than yours!'
Mussolini and Rimet
compare their World Cup
trophies.

The 1930 Cup Final referee John Langenus later said that most countries regarded the tournament as a sporting fiasco, 'because beside the desire to win, all other sporting considerations were non-existent, and because, moreover, a certain spirit brooded over the whole championship. Italy wanted to win, it was natural, but they allowed it to be seen too clearly.'

Nobbled referees

Inevitably, perhaps, there were suspicions that referees had been got at. After all, Mussolini had hand-picked them.

In the drawn quarter-final match against Spain (refereed by the Belgian Louis Baert) the Italian forward Giovanni Ferrari was allowed to equalise despite the fact that the goalkeeper was clearly being obstructed – and was so badly mauled throughout that he couldn't take part in the replay. The Swiss referee René Mercet, who took charge of that game (1–0 to Italy), gave the hosts so much licence that he was banned by his own FA when he returned home.

Italy beat Austria 1–0 in their semi-final, after which the Austrian striker Josef Bican complained that the referee (Ivan Eklind of Sweden) had 'played' for the opposition – though of course we do have to allow for a possible helping of sour grapes.

'When I passed the ball out to the right wing,' he said, 'one of our players, Cicek, ran for it and the referee headed it back to the Italians. It was unbelievable!'

STATS CARD

Refereed most matches (8):

Joël Quiniou, France (1986–1994)
Benito Archundia, Mexico (2006–2010)
Jorge Larrionda, Uruguay (2006–2010)

**Most matches refereed
in one tournament (5):**

Benito Archundia, Mexico (2006)
Horacio Elizondo, Argentina (2006)
Ravshan Irmatov, Uzbekistan (2010)

More of the same

If the 1934 tournament was played under the shadow of Fascism, the 1938 World Cup added the black clouds of impending war.

In the intervening years Mussolini's forces had swept into Ethiopia, dropping poisonous mustard gas, destroying villages and killing prisoners. Hitler had tightened his grip on the Third Reich and had annexed neighbouring Austria in the so-called Anschluss.

What would FIFA do about this? Why, invite them to the next World Cup finals in Paris, of course. The show must go on!

Oh, and Germany were allowed to select the best Austrian players for their team – as they were very pleased to do.

In Spain, meanwhile, another Fascist regime under General Franco was engaged in a bloody civil war against its Republican adversaries. They couldn't very well send a team, but would doubtless have been welcomed with open arms if they had.

The fallout of war

Two World Cup captains later lost their lives because of the sharply contrasting things they did in the war:

- **Alexandre Villaplane**, the right-half who captained France in the 1930 finals, was executed by the Resistance on Boxing Day 1944. He'd been a leader of a criminal organisation which had collaborated with the Nazis in anti-Resistance activities.

- **Milutin Ivkovic**, the Serbian right-back who captained Yugoslavia in the same tournament, was part of a group which demanded a boycott of the 1936 Berlin Olympics for political reasons and was among those responsible for the withdrawal of the Yugoslavian team. He was arrested by the Gestapo several times during the war, and was shot to death in Jajici Concentration Camp in May, 1943.

1938

- **Host country:** France.

- **Finalists:** Belgium, Brazil, Czechoslovakia, Cuba, Dutch East Indies, France, Germany, Holland, Hungary, Italy, Norway, Poland, Romania, Sweden, Switzerland.

- **What happened:** Argentina declined to take part, piqued that they weren't hosting the tournament – it *was* South America's turn – and Uruguay stayed away again.

  Austria (annexed by Germany), and Spain (involved in a civil war), were also missing. As Austria had dropped out after qualifying (and England had declined FIFA's invitation to replace them) there were only 15 teams competing, and Sweden were given a bye in the first round.

  Italy narrowly survived their opening match against Norway, but then dispatched France and Brazil before beating Hungary 4–2 in the Final.

- **Champions:** Italy.

- **What happened next:** Germany invaded Czechoslovakia and Poland, war was declared, and the World Cup would not be held again until 1950.

Mussolini no longer had the home advantage, but that didn't stop him throwing his weight around. The team coach, Vittorio Pozzo, later said that he'd been told to include only Fascist sympathisers in his team, and there were ructions when, in the first match of the tournament against Norway (which they almost lost), the ageing Eraldo Monzeglio was picked in defence instead of the young star Alfredo Foni.

Not only the ref needed them!

Several players have worn glasses in World Cup tournaments, the first of them being Leopoldi Kielholz, who in 1934 scored twice for Switzerland in their opening match against Holland.

Two bespectacled captains were Fraans Meeng of the Dutch East Indies in 1938 and South Korea's Park KC in 1954, while the most recent example was the combative Dutch midfield Edgar Davids, who played in the 1998 finals in France. Unable to wear contact lenses because of glaucoma, he became well known for his stylish wrap-around goggles.

This time, apparently, it was nothing to do with politics – Monzeglio was a favourite at the dictator's mansion, where he coached the Duce and his sons, and Mussolini had ordered his inclusion in the side. The president of Italy's football federation intervened (bravely, you'd have thought) and Foni played in all the remaining games.

Black Shirts

There were large contingents of belligerent anti-Fascists in the crowds, with an estimated 10,000 Italian exiles in the ground for the Norway game. They barracked, howled and whistled when the Italians gave the straight-arm salute, and the wily Pozzo reacted immediately: 'We had just put our hands down when the demonstration started again,' he said. 'Straight away – "Team be ready: salute!" And we raised our hands again to confirm we had no fear. Having won the battle of intimidation, we played.'

Against France in the quarter-finals the Italians made a crudely provocative gesture. As both teams usually wore blue tops, Italy had to switch to another colour. This would normally have been white, but – you've guessed it – they ran onto the pitch wearing black shirts.

When the Germans, including their five Austrian internationals, gave Nazi salutes before the tournament's opening match against Switzerland at the Parc des Princes Stadium in Paris, some of the protestors went so far as to throw broken bottles in their direction.

Three weeks earlier England had played Germany in a friendly in Berlin (no moral superiority there, then), and its players had obediently – out of courtesy, they would say – raised their arms to the skies.

Not so the Swiss. The players kept their arms resolutely by their sides – and then proceeded to knock their opponents out of the championship 4–2 in a replay.

The Germans would all too soon be back in Paris – but not playing football.

Out in the cold

The new international order after the war couldn't help but affect the World Cup. Germany, who had applied to stage the 1942 championship (who did you think you were kidding, Mr Hitler?) were banned from the first post-war tournament in 1950 – a rare FIFA rap over the knuckles.

There was now a Cold War stand-off between the western democracies and the communist countries of the Soviet Union (USSR). It wouldn't be long before the eastern bloc used sport as a propaganda tool – don't even think about all those muscular women weight-lifters and shot-putters – but their footballers didn't return to the world stage until 1954.

STATS CARD

Youngest and oldest referees:

24 years, 193 days old: Juan Gardeazabal, Spain 1958

53 years, 236 days old: George Reader, England 1950

The Brits arrive

It had taken them twenty years, but ahead of the 1950 World Cup in Brazil the four British associations (England, Scotland, Wales and Northern Ireland) at last applied to take part. They were put in their own play-off group with the top two going through. Scotland, however, said they'd only travel if they came first, and they were beaten into second place by England.

England's squad included such greats as Stanley Matthews, Tom Finney and Jackie Milburn, but they famously lost 1–0 to the United States and were soon on their way home.
So who was the first Englishman to appear in a World Cup final? George Reader, the referee, that's who!

England
joins in
at last –
modestly

1950

- **Host country:** Brazil.

- **Finalists:** Bolivia, Brazil, Chile, England, Italy, Mexico, Paraguay, Spain, Sweden, Switzerland, Uruguay, USA, Yugoslavia.

- **What happened:** As in 1930, only 13 mismatched teams took part. Germany were banned because of the war. Italy took part, but its squad had been severely depleted by the 1949 air crash which killed every member of the brilliant Torino team.

  Brazil were the clear favourites, partly because of their skill but also because many of the other teams had to fly huge distances between matches.

  The tournament was organised on a pool basis, ending with a final league table rather than a proper Final. However, the last game pitched Brazil (4 points) against Uruguay (3 points) – so it became, in effect, a Cup Final after all. Uruguay came from behind at the newly built Maracanã stadium to win 2–1.

- **Champions:** Uruguay.

- **What happened next:** Brazilian fans disgracefully blamed the black members of the team for their defeat.

Magyar misery

By this time Hungary were the masters – the Mighty Magyars – with an all-conquering team that included Puskas, Czibor, Kocsis and Hidegkuti. They surprisingly lost 3–2 to West Germany in the 1954 Final, after being two goals up in the first eight minutes, and they were immediately treated as traitors by the country's political leaders. Their great goalkeeper Gyula Grosics later recalled that what was to have been a ceremonial dinner on their return home 'was more like a funeral feast, and I felt that Hungarian football was being buried'.

The general secretary of the Hungarian Communist Party (the country's most powerful politician) told them there would be no consequences as a result of their defeat, and they knew enough of communist double-speak to know what the assurance meant: 'Of course we knew right away that we had to fear.'

That November Grosics was ordered off the pitch just before a league match. The following January, with nothing having been said to him in the meantime, he was summoned to the Ministry of Defence and told that he faced a charge of espionage, a crime which carried the death sentence.

All this for losing a football match!

Grosics was as suddenly and inexplicably allowed to play football again as he had been barred from doing so in the first place, but much worse was to follow.

STATS CARD

Fastest World Cup goals (in seconds):

10.89 Hakan Sukur, Turkey v Korea, 2002
15 Václav Masek, Czechoslovakia v Mexico, 1962
25 Ernst Lehner, Germany v Austria, 1934
28 Bryan Robson, England v France, 1982
31 Bernard Lacombe, France v Italy, 1978
35 Émile Veinante, France v Belgium, 1938
35 Arne Nyberg, Sweden v Hungary, 1938
50 Adalbert Desu, Romania v Peru, 1930
50 Flórián Albert, Hungary v Bulgaria, 1962
50 Pak Seung-Jin, N. Korea v Portugal, 1966
52 Celso Ayala, Paraguay v Nigeria, 1998

An uprising

In October 1956 there was a popular uprising against Hungary's Stalinist rulers, and the government fell – at which point the Soviet Politburo decided to send in Russian tanks, with dire consequences:

- **More than 2,500 Hungarians were killed.**
- **Some 700 Soviet troops also lost their lives.**
- **200,000 Hungarians fled, to become refugees.**

Sport fades into insigificance at times like this, but there were inevitably consequences for the outstanding Hungarians who had brought the world a new dynamic brand of football.

Grosics, Puskas, Czibor and Kocsis were all out of the country, touring with the leading club team Honvéd, when the revolution and its bloody suppression took place. They accepted a tour of Brazil, but the Hungarian FA banned it, and it was called off.

Why? Grosics again: 'FIFA had agreed with the Hungarian FA, and the leading Honvéd players were banned.'

Several of those players chose to live and play overseas after the failed revolution. Grosics himself returned, and he was in goal on 17 June 1958 when his much depleted team were knocked out of the next World Cup by Wales.

The atmosphere was dreadful, because on the previous day, after a secret trial, the leader of the 1956 uprising, Imre Nagy, had been executed by hanging. Free Hungary protesters kept up their chants throughout the game and draped black banners over the stands. Did the result really matter?

A black and white issue

FIFA presidents have a lot of clout, and Sir Stanley Rous's handling of the apartheid issue shows just how influential they can be.

Opposition to the black/white race divide in South Africa – with all the money and power on the white side – was what we would today call a 'no-brainer'. All the other African countries were against this inhumane policy, and in 1958 South Africa was expelled from the African Cup of Nations.

A public forum

Politicians may have used the World Cup to their own advantage over the years, but the huge coverage given to matches, with 'live' pictures beamed across the world, has also allowed both fans and players to make protests of their own. Here are two examples:

1982 When Poland played the USSR in Spain for a place in the semi-finals, their supporters waved banners supporting the trade union Solidarity, whose leader, Lech Wałęsa, would later become the country's president.

Spanish police brutally removed them – it's thought in response to a request by Soviet television.

2009 When Iran played a qualifying match against South Korea in Seoul six of their players wore green wristbands to show their solidarity with the Iranian opposition candidate Mir Hossein Mousavi   .

Most of the players obeyed instructions to remove the bands at half-time, but the captain, Mehdi Mahdavikia, wore his captain's green armband for the rest of the match.

The authorities responded by imposing life bans on Mahdavikia and three of this teammates – Ali Karimi, Hosein Ka'abi and Vahid Hashemian. Their gesture had been seen on television all around the world.

The all-white Football Association of South Africa joined FIFA that same year, but it was formally suspended in 1961 because it had failed to fall in line with the organisation's non-discriminatory regulations.

So far so obvious – but then Sir Stanley, the English FA's president, took over at the helm of FIFA and said it shouldn't 'embroil itself in political matters'. Well, it had stood back from condemning Mussolini, hadn't it? He was at least being consistent.

Diplomatic protests

Some countries have used the World Cup to make political points – even though it cost them a potential place in the finals. For example:

1970 North Korea told FIFA that they wouldn't play an away match in Israel.

1978 The Soviet Union refused to take part in a play-off in Chile's Estadio Nacional because it had been used to hold General Pinochet's opponents, many of whom were murdered.

India had another reason for withdrawing in 1950: FIFA wouldn't let them play in bare feet!

Sir Stanley now took himself off to investigate the state of football in South Africa, and he came back saying that there was a real danger that football would fold there, 'possibly to the point of no recovery', if its football association was thrown out of FIFA. Therefore it must stay in – and in January 1963 its suspension was lifted.

Fortunately this head-in-the-sand attitude wasn't to prevail for long. Suitably angered, representatives of football associations across Africa and Asia turned up in large numbers to FIFA's 1964 conference, emphatically re-imposing South Africa's suspension.

Twelve years later, after the authorities had bloodily put down an uprising in the Johannesburg township of Soweto, South Africa was expelled from FIFA altogether, and would remain in the wilderness for another 15 years until it changed its ways.

And did this severity kill off South African football as Sir Stanley had so gloomily predicted? Tell that to the people charged with organising the 2010 World Cup!

The football war

George Orwell described sport as 'war minus the shooting', but he died nearly twenty years before Honduras and El Salvador combined the two.

Of course the so-called 'football war' wasn't just (or even mainly) about football, but the three matches the two neighbouring Central American countries played in the World Cup play-offs in June, 1969, inflamed passions which had been smouldering for years.

Honduras had by far the greater landmass, but El Salvador had the larger population – and over the years some 300,000 of its poorer people had crossed the border to farm in Honduras.

STATS CARD

Most goals scored in World Cup finals:
201 Brazil

Fewest:
0 Canada, China PR, Indonesia (as Dutch East Indies), Trinidad and Tobago, Congo DR (as Zaire)

1954

FACT FILE

- **Host country:** Switzerland.

- **Finalists:** Austria, Belgium, Brazil, Czechoslovakia, England, France, Hungary, Italy, Mexico, Scotland, South Korea, Switzerland, Turkey, Uruguay, West Germany, Yugoslavia.

- **What happened:** The first televised World Cup, it retained the mini-league system but in the first round each group of four had two seeds who would play only the two non-seeds.

  Hungary were the overwhelming favourites, having beaten several decent teams convincingly and having famously become the first foreign side to win in England, 6–3.

  They coasted to the Final, beating South Korea 9–0, West Germany 8–3 and Uruguay 4–2. Playing the Germans again in the Final, they led 2–0 but lost 3–2.

- **Champions:** West Germany.

- **What happened next:** In the aftermath of the Hungarian uprising many of its team emigrated, and the country was never a footballing power again .

With Honduran peasants demanding more land of their own, its government decided to dispossess the immigrant Salvadorans – who wouldn't be welcomed home in such huge numbers. Tensions were running very high.

The death of a 'martyr'

When the El Salvador team arrived for the first match in the Honduran capital, Tegucigalpa, they were greeted in the traditional way – that is, they were kept awake all night by the locals, who threw stones at their hotel windows, set off firecrackers and beat sticks on tin sheets.

Next day the weary players lost the match to a last-minute goal, at which point an 18-year-old Salvadoran supporter, Amelia Bolaños, crossed the room from her television set, took her father's revolver from a drawer and shot herself through the heart.

Cue the worst kind of emotional drum-beating. The Salvadoran newspaper *El Nacional* reported that 'the young girl could not bear to see her fatherland brought to its knees'. Her funeral was televised, with an army honour guard marching at the head of the procession and the president of the republic and his ministers walking behind a flag-draped coffin. The Salvadoran football team, fresh back from a vicious send-off at the airport in Honduras, brought up the rear.

The second game was preceded by the inevitable tit-for-tat. This time the Honduran team was kept awake by screaming crowds, who broke their windows and threw all manner of things inside, including dead rats. The players were taken to the match in armoured cars, while Salvadoran fans lined the route waving pictures of the virtually sanctified Amelia Bolaños.

At the ground the Honduran flag was burned to widespread joy, and (as an extra insult) a dirty dishcloth was run up the pole in its place. After the visitors went down 3–0, their coach commented 'We're very lucky that we lost.'

Some foolishly brave Honduran fans had crossed the border to support their team. They were now savagely attacked, and two of them were killed. As many as 150 of their cars

It wasn't just temperatures that ran high between El Salvador and Honduras.

were burned, and a few hours later the border between the two countries was closed.

Mercifully, the decider was played on neutral territory, in Mexico, where five thousand Mexican police stationed themselves between the two sets of fans. (For the record, El Salvador won 3–2 with a goal in extra time. They were to be knocked out in the finals the following summer without scoring a goal.)

The war, by now inevitable, was a brief and somewhat ramshackle affair. It's notable for being the last to be fought with piston-engined fighters, because both sides commandeered US aircraft from the Second World War and the Korean War. On the ground there was often confusion in border skirmishes, because the two armies not only spoke the same language but were dressed in identical army gear.

STATS CARD

Most finals matches played without a win or a draw:

6 El Salvador

It was all over within a hundred days, but it had taken a heavy toll:

- 6,000 people were killed.
- More than 12,000 were wounded.
- 50,000 lost their homes and fields.
- Many villages were destroyed.

Another dictator...

We'll stay on the American continent a little while longer to wallow in the tournament staged in Argentina in the summer of 1978.

Consider: the hosts had been awarded these finals twelve years before, but quite a lot had happened in the meantime. Specifically, in March 1976 there had been a military coup, and the new regime in Argentina was conducting a brutal policy (the so-called Dirty War) of eliminating its political opponents.

Men, women and children, most of them innocent of any crime whatsoever, were being taken to secret detention centres where they were tortured, after which thousands of them vanished without trace – the *desaparecidos*.

In these appalling circumstances FIFA had to make a decision, and it surely won't surprise you to learn what that decision was: *The show must go on.* Several countries threatened a boycott – and international stars such as Sepp Maier and Paolo Rossi signed petitions of protest against Argentina's treatment of its political prisoners – but they all swallowed their distaste in order to join the circus.

Passarella's handshake

For many observers the worst moment of the World Cup was seeing the trophy being presented by General Videla. The Argentina captain Daniel Passarella later told his own anti-regime story about greeting the dictator in the dressing room after the game. He was, to put it delicately, soaping his underparts when the general arrived. Passarella said of the incident:

'He had to shake hands with me with all the photographers and journalists there, and then he pulled a face! It was all very funny, but I had to go abroad to play afterwards. I am very proud of what I did, and I don't regret it.'

What a splendid opportunity for General Jorge Videla to give his cruel junta a superficial gloss! He spent more than $700,000 on the tournament, and hired the leading US public relations firm Burston–Marstella to promote the country as being a haven of prosperity and humanity.

Just in case anyone looked too hard the regime bulldozed shanty towns on the edges of the major cities where the matches were to be staged, while in Rosario a wall was erected along the main road so that visitors wouldn't see the slums behind.

The publicity worked both ways, however. The full horror of what the Argentinian regime was up to hadn't sunk in around the world before the finals, and Amnesty International made sure that journalists bound for Buenos Aires were given evidence of the state-sponsored atrocities being committed there.

There was a weird incident in France, when – shortly before the squad flew to South America – the national team coach, Michel Hidalgo, apparently foiled a kidnap attempt by a group protesting about French involvement with the Argentinian regime. Three men stopped his car north of Bordeaux, but Hidalgo managed to wrestle their gun away from them and speed away to safety.

And there was some welcome publicity for the Mothers of the Plaza de Mayo protesters, whose sons and daughters had been taken away in the night and had never returned.

… and one more

Now fast-forward four years to 1982. The World Cup was being held in Spain, and the Argentinian junta, with its death squads still operating, remained in power under General Leopoldo Galtieri.

A little more than two months earlier Galtieri had ordered the occupation of the small outcrop in the South Atlantic which the Argentinians know as Las Malvinas and the British (who had declared sovereignty back in 1833) as the Falkland Islands. The writer Jorge Luis Borges described the ensuing war as 'two bald men fighting over a comb'.

Argentina, as holders, launched the tournament on 13 April (a 1–0 defeat to Belgium), their players not realising that the war was all but over: their army commander would formally surrender the next day.

Ossie Ardiles, the elegant Argentine midfielder who played for Tottenham Hotspur in England and had to give up an FA Cup Final appearance and fly home because of the conflict, later revealed that 'things were not quite how we had been told'. The defeat was a shock, 'because when we left Argentina we were winning the war and when we arrived in Spain we were already losing it, according to the Spanish and English newspapers'.

Why hadn't they known? Well, this was just another case of the politicians using the World Cup for their own ends. The invasion itself had been a smokescreen to cover the regime's growing unpopularity, and Galtieri had stoked up a frenzy of optimism about both the Malvinas invasion and the forthcoming tournament. Both campaigns ended in defeat, and Galtieri was swiftly ousted by another military junta.

Playing the race card

Let's end this saga of blatant political gamesmanship with another attempt that went emphatically wrong.

When France hosted the tournament in 1998 the far-right National Front leader Jean-Marie Le Pen seized the opportunity of attacking the country's immigration policy by criticising the multiracial mix of the French national team. The 'foreign' players, he alleged, didn't know the words of the French national anthem, and to call the squad French was a sham.

STATS CARD

Most appearances in finals:

25 Lothar Matthaeus, Germany
1982–1998 (2,052 minutes)
23 Paolo Maldini, Italy
1990–2002 (2,217 minutes)
21 Uwe Seeler, Germany
1958–1970 (1,980 minutes)
21 Wladislaw Zmuda, Poland
1974–1986 (1,808 minutes)
21 Diego Maradona, Argentina
1982–1994 (1,938 minutes)

1958

FACT FILE

- **Host country:** Sweden.

- **Finalists:** Argentina, Austria, Brazil, Czechoslovakia, England, France, Hungary, Mexico, Northern Ireland, Paraguay, Scotland, Sweden, USSR, Wales, West Germany, Yugoslavia.

- **What happened:** For the first time in the World Cup finals there were no seeds. The Hungarians were without Puskas and other leading players in the aftermath of the 1956 uprising. Britain had four representatives for the first time, but the English and Northern Ireland squads were depleted because of the Munich air crash which had killed several of their Manchester United players.

  The tournament was notable for the emergence of the 17-year-old Pelé, who scored six goals without appearing in the first two matches. He scored two in the Final, in which Brazil beat the hosts 5-2.

- **Champions:** Brazil.

- **What happened next:** The 4-2-4 playing formation adopted by Brazil in Sweden quickly spread through world football.

This was no doubt less than amusing for the likes of Michel Desailly, Patrick Vieira and Christian Karembeu (born in French African colonies), Lilian Thuram (from the Caribbean), Youri Djorkaeff and Alain Boghossian (ethnic Armenians), Fabien Barthez (the grandson of Spaniards), Bixente Lizarazu (a Basque) and Zinedine Zidane, born to Algerian parents.

Djorkaeff pointed out that the accusation wasn't true anyway: 'Of the 22 players nearly 20 had been in the French army, and that's where people learn *La Marseillaise*. So we all knew it and we sang it before each match.'

Thierry Henry described Le Pen's comment as 'cheap talk', adding that 'everybody was proud to be French'.

The French public soon had reason to be pretty proud, too, because France swept through to the Final, where they beat Brazil 3–0. Two of the goals were scored by the charismatic Zidane, who was paid the ultimate tribute when, that night, his face and the words 'Merci Zizou' (his nickname) were projected onto the Arc de Triomphe in Paris as a million fans congregated in the Champs Elysées to celebrate.

Le Pen was forced into an embarrassing and unconvincing revision of his earlier comments. He'd always recognised that France should be composed of different races and religions, he said, as long as they displayed the right amount of patriotism.

So a notable victory for football over political opportunism – and a rare one. After all, many of the fans were unable to forget that after France beat Croatia at the Stade de France to reach the Final, President Jacques Chirac (never known for a love of football) had shamelessly tried to cover himself with glory by putting on a Number 23 shirt and mixing with the players in front of the cameras.

No, you simply can't keep these characters down!

CHAPTER TWO

OVER THE TOP

Politicians are fair game, but there's no point in pretending that they alone have corrupted world football.

Remember Bill Shankly's joke about the game being more important than life and death? An awful lot of people seem to have believed it.

Orwell again: 'Serious sport has nothing to do with fair play. It is bound up with hatred, jealousy, boastfulness, disregard of all rules and sadistic pleasure in witnessing violence.'

Welcome to the World Cup, George!

This chapter brings you a rich catalogue of 'over the top' behaviour – by fans a bit too fanatical for comfort; by players happy to break an opponent's leg; by match-fixers, drug-takers, fast-buck merchants... It's an impressively long list of scoundrels.

In the beginning...

The seeds of all this were sown in the very first tournament. For instance, Montevideo 1930 had the original hard man in Luisito Monti, an Argentina defender who's been described by the writer Cris Freddi in alarming terms: 'Desperate Dan jaw, no neck and legs that went right through a man.' We get the picture.

STATS CARD

Fastest sendings-off:

0'56" José Batista, Uruguay v Scotland 1986
3' Marco Etcheverry, Bolivia v Germany 1994
3' Ion Vladoui, Romania v Switzerland 1994
3' Morten Wieghorst, Denmark v South Africa 1998
6' Lauren, Cameroon v Chile 1998

He made a cripple of one of his opponents in the second minute of Argentina's opening game against France – and later, to rub salt into the wound as it were, scored the only goal of the match.

It's a strange fact that Monti, having appeared as a losing finalist in 1930, carried out his 'search and destroy' tactics for Italy when they won the next World Cup, the rules allowing him to switch national teams because of his Italian ancestry.

That first World Cup also had its fair share of intimidation. Just before the Final, Monti received a death threat, which he evidently took seriously. And why not? When thousands of Argentine fans had flocked onto packetboats the previous evening to be ferried across the River Plate for the match, huge crowds roared 'Victory or death!' amid a cacophany of fireworks.

On the big day itself the fans were frisked for revolvers both at the customs post and at the stadium. The huge new ground was already packed out by noon, hours ahead of kick-off.

Given the brush-off

Losing has never been taken lightly by South Americans, but the brilliant Brazilian goalkeeper Moacyr Barbosa suffered more than most after his team (the favourites, and playing at home) lost to Uruguay in the 1950 Final.

Despite being voted by journalists as the best keeper in the tournament, he was soon hounded from the game, ending up as a cleaner at the Maracanã stadium.

Thirteen years after the defeat he was offered the goalposts as a souvenir. He took them home, invited his friends to a barbecue – and burnt the posts to cinders.

The Brazilians brought on their new sweeper.

Soldiers with fixed bayonets patrolled the perimeter while the Argentinian squad arrived under police guard, having been given protection day and night.

And how would you have fancied being the poor referee? John Langenus demanded that the authorities guarantee safety for himself and his linesmen, and once he'd blown the final whistle he made a swift escape to his waiting boat along a pre-arranged route.

The following day, naturally enough, was declared a national holiday in Uruguay. In Buenos Aires, meanwhile, police opened fire as an angry mob stoned the Uruguayan embassy. For good measure the two football associations broke off relations with one another. What a great start!

Bad manners

For those of us who've imagined playing in a World Cup match (hands up if you haven't) there can be no sensation greater than scoring the winning goal and soaking up the adulation of the crowd.

Few of us, surely, would dream of displaying our nastiest side in front of the world's cameras – and yet international players have done that over and over again. Here are a few random examples:

- **1974.** During a match between Germany and Australia in Hamburg the home fans disliked their team's negative approach, and Franz Beckenbauer was abused when he gave the ball away. He spat at the crowd.

- **1986.** Iraq defender Samir Shaker Mahmoud was obviously less than happy about his side's 2–1 defeat against Belgium. He spat at the referee – and earned himself a one-year ban.

- **1990.** In a second-round match between West Germany and Holland, the Dutch midfielder Frank Rijkaard was booked for a nasty foul on Rudi Völler, but Völler's name also went into the book when he complained that Rijkaard had spat in his hair. A little later both were sent off, and Rijkaard now spat twice in Völler's face.

- **1994.** When Stefan Effenberg was substituted in the game against South Korea, the German fans barracked him. He responded with an obscene gesture, and was promptly sent home by his coach, Berti Vogts.

Hurt feelings

To get involved in a playground spat in the World Cup Final itself is taking self-destruction to the extreme, but that's what the French captain Zinedine Zidane did against Italy in 2006. The worst thing for his team-mates was that the game was on a knife-edge at 1–1 in extra time: they'd soon lose on penalties with Zidane, their specialist, a mere spectator.

'Little Bird' flies free

Missing the next game for being sent off wasn't an obligatory punishment back in 1962 and, in truth, the foul which saw 'Little Bird' Garrincha sent off for Brazil in the semi-final against Chile (in response to being spat at) was pretty tame.

Nevertheless it was a little strange that Garrincha's sending-off seems not to have appeared in the referee's match report, and that the Uruguayan player involved rapidly returned to Montevideo and wasn't called to give evidence. Garrincha scored twice in the Final.

And what was it all about? Zidane apparently had his shirt pulled by the defender Marco Materazzi and told him he could have it after the final whistle. The Italian's story was that he then made a crude remark about Zidane's sister (although he didn't know that he actually had one!), at which point the Frenchman head-butted him in the chest. It was Zidane's last action in professional football, but he walked away with the Golden Ball as the tournament's best player – the voting having already been completed at half-time.

Winding up an individual player is one thing. It takes some doing to incense a whole nation...

STATS CARD

Referees giving most red cards:

6 Arturo Brizio Carter, Mexico, 1994–1998
5 Joël Quiniou, France, 1986–1994
4 Jamal Al Sharif, Syria, 1986–1994
4 Felipe Ramos Rizo, Mexico, 2002
4 Graham Poll, England, 2006
4 Valentin Ivanov, Russia, 2006

Before the 1962 finals in Chile two Italian journalists, Antonio Ghirelli and Corrado Pizzinelli, wrote articles about the poverty of Santiago and the supposed loose morals of its women. They wisely left the country before the tournament began, but you can probably imagine what happened when the two teams met. (*Check it out by turning the page.*)

The match wasn't the only thing about to kick off.

The dirtiest matches ever

Here are four slug-fests which have gone down (heavily) in World Cup history:

The Battle of Bordeaux
Brazil 1 – Czechoslovakia 1, 12 June 1938

The Hungarian Paul von Hertzka refereed this quarter-final, sending off Zezé Procópio after only 14 minutes and both Arthur Machado and Jan Riha just before half-time. A great deal of pushing and shoving went unpunished, and at one stage there were bodies strewn all over the pitch. The Czech keeper and captain Frantisek Plánicka broke an arm and Oldrich Nejedly (who scored the Czech goal from the penalty spot) broke a leg.

The Battle of Berne
Hungary 4 – Brazil 2, 27 June 1954

The English referee Arthur Ellis sent off two Brazilians and a Hungarian in the last twenty minutes – Bozsik and Nilton Santos together (there were allegations of racial abuse) and Humberto for jumping on Kocsis with what was later described as 'one tremendous leap'.

Other ferocious tackles went unpunished, there was a punch-up at the final whistle and some reports say Puskas cut open an opponent's head with a bottle. Glass was thrown into the Hungarian changing room, where the lights went out and a bloodied player had to be treated by a doctor.

The Battle of Santiago
Chile 2 – Italy 0, 2 June 1962

Incensed by the reports by two Italian journalists (*page 75*), the Chilean crowd bayed for blood and their players were spitting in the Italians' faces straight from the kick-off.

Once again an English referee was involved, and Ken Aston doesn't seem to have made a good job of it. He did nothing when Giorgio Ferrini and Leonel Sánchez kicked one another, then sent Ferrini off for retaliation – and it took the police eight minutes to get him off the pitch. Sánchez flattened Mario David with a punch in front of a linesman and got away with it, so David kicked him in the neck and *was* sent off.

Jorge Toro wrestled Bruno Mora to the ground, but although Aston tugged them apart he sent no-one off. And someone unknown broke Humberto Maschio's nose.

The Battle of Nuremberg
Portugal 1 – Holland 0, 25 June 2006

This match broke a World Cup record, with the Russian referee, Valentin Ivanov, issuing a record 16 yellow cards and four reds (two for each team). There were countless fouls, a head-butt by Portugal's Figo which should have resulted in a red rather than the yellow he got, and a mass brawl when the Dutch declined to give the ball back after Portugal had put it out for an injured player to receive attention.

1962

- **Host country:** Chile.

- **Finalists:** Argentina, Brazil, Bulgaria, Czechoslovakia, Chile, Columbia, England, Hungary, Italy, Mexico, Spain, Switzerland, Uruguay, USSR, West Germany, Yugoslavia.

- **What happened:** There were four groups of four, but if teams were level on points goal average (later goal difference) would be used to separate them.

  Brazil were the favourites to keep their title, although Pelé was injured early in the tournament and was unable to continue. (Garrincha was their star player). Italy were in their highly defensive 'catenaccio' phase and went out in the first round.

  Brazil beat Czechoslovakia 3–1 in the Final after being a goal down.

- **Champions:** Brazil.

- **What happened next:** Let's be provincial: Walter Winterbottom stood down as England's manager and was replaced by Alf Ramsey.

You won't be surprised to learn that the Italian players were stoned at their training camp. In fact the 1962 World Cup was one of the most violent of them all, with no fewer than 34 serious injuries in just three match days, and the following tournament was also blatantly rugged, with Pelé having to retire hurt after a succession of cynical tackles left him hobbling.

Scum of the earth

England's Alf Ramsey, after a bruising quarter-final against Argentina in 1966, said their opponents had behaved 'like animals' – a comment which helped maintain a keen rivalry between the two countries for years afterwards. (He also tried to prevent his players swapping shirts with the opposition after the game.)

The secretary of the Scottish FA, Ernie Walker, was similarly incensed after his team played out a crudely contested goalless draw with Uruguay in 1986. He went so far as to say that Scotland had been playing against 'the scum of world football'.

Others have been more philosophical. After Luis Figo had head-butted an opponent in the notorious 'Battle of Nuremberg' (page 77), the Portugal manager Luiz Felipe Scolari remarked with a shrug that 'Jesus Christ may be able to turn the other cheek, but Luis Figo isn't Jesus Christ.'

Give that ref a yellow!

Sepp Blatter, FIFA's president, knew what he thought about that bar-room brawl of a match. His immediate comment – although he apologised later – was that the referee should have given *himself* a yellow card for the way he'd handled it.

A surprising reaction? Not really. In 1998 FIFA asked referees to send players off for violent conduct. In a first-round match between Denmark and South Africa the Colombian referee Toro Rendón duly (and rightly) sent off three players in a match between Denmark and South Africa – and was rewarded for his obedience by being immediately dropped from the tournament.

And how apologetic do you think Harald Schumacher was about his horrendous foul on Battiston (below) in 1982? Not very, it seems, because he later coldly offered to pay to have the Frenchman's teeth capped.

But here's a welcome exception to prove the rule. In 1994 Italy's Mauro Tassotti elbowed Luis Enrique of Spain in the face in the quarter-final. He wasn't booked at the time, but he was later banned for eight matches – and he never played for his country again.

The nastiest foul?

A close call because there have been too many, but nobody who saw German goalkeeper Harald Schumacher's clattering of Patrick Battiston in the 1982 semi-final between Germany and France can recall it without wincing. With the score at 1–1 Battiston raced onto a through ball and reached it first – whereupon Schumacher launched himself forward, forearm raised, and smashed him to the ground.

The Frenchman, heavily concussed, lost two teeth. No penalty was awarded by the Dutch referee Charles Corver, and the Germans went on to win the match in a penalty shoot-out.

Not really trying

Breaking limbs to win a crucial match is one thing: not really trying to win at all is a different one altogether. Why should players not bother?

That's the question Brazilian fans were asking in 1978. A league table operated in the second round, and Argentina – the host nation – knew

One player – three yellows

The English referee Graham Poll had his hopes of officiating at the 2006 Final dashed by a strange mistake in the group match between Australia and Croatia. Immediately after the final whistle he was pushed angrily by the Croatian Josip Simunic. Poll produced what he thought was his second yellow for Simunic and therefore raised the red card, too. What he didn't realise was that this was the Croatian's *third* yellow: he should have received his marching orders for the second one, just before full time. In the aftermath of the debacle, Poll retired from international refereeing.

when they kicked off against Peru that they had to win by three clear goals and score at least four in order to take a place in the Final at Brazil's expense.

Peru had lost 3–0 to Brazil and 1–0 to Poland, so they certainly weren't high-flyers. This time they were 4–0 down within 50 minutes and finally lost, abjectly, 6-0. Of course, since this was the World Cup, there was talk of bribery and corruption, but it has to be said that no genuine evidence has ever emerged to support this theory.

The Peruvian goalkeeper Ramón Quiroga was in a particularly uncomfortable position because he was a naturalised Argentinian, and after the match he went so far as to publish an open letter defending himself and his team-mates.

During the next World Cup, in Spain, it was the turn of Algerian fans to ask questions. They watched in disbelief as West Germany and Austria played out a farce of a match in which it didn't suit either side to score a goal once West Germany had taken an early lead.

Why? Because as things then stood West Germany and Austria would proceed to the next round with a better goal difference than Algeria, who had the same number of points. This meant that 1–0 was a positive result for both teams.

Again, there's no evidence of a pre-agreed result, but you can understand the fury of the Algerian supporters (who waved banknotes through the wire fencing to show what *they* thought was going on) as the endless minutes ticked by with neither side bothering to make a serious attack.

It wasn't only the Algerians, either. A German TV commentator told viewers, 'What's hapening here is disgraceful and has nothing to do with football', while the next morning Germany's best-selling tabloid newspaper carried a 'Shame On You' headline. And when fans turned up outside the hotel where the German team was staying they contemptuously pelted the team with water-filled balloons. 'We wanted to progress,' explained their coach, Jupp Derwall, 'not play football.'

fritz was looking
forward to wearing his
new goalkeeping gloves.

The one positive thing to come out of this no-show was a FIFA rule that deciding matches in a tournament must in future be played at the same time so that no team should have an unfair advantage over another.

A rocket for Roberto

And then there was the attempt of Chile goalkeeper Roberto Rojas to get a match called off. In a 1989 qualifier against Brazil at the Maracanã, Chile needed to win by two goals – and at 1–0 down with twenty minutes left they obviously weren't going to make it.

A Brazilian fan named Rosemary de Mello had thrown a firework from the stands, and when the referee saw Rojas writhing on the ground close to it and clutching his head in his hands

---

STATS CARD

Fastest substitutions (in minutes):

4 Alessandro Nesta, Italy v Austria 1998
4 Bryan Robson, England v Morocco 1986
4 Michael Owen, England v Sweden 2006
6 Mauro Bellugi, Italy v Argentina 1978

---

he obviously feared the worst: he had a badly injured player to deal with. Closer inspection revealed that the keeper had a bloody wound, and he was immediately stretchered off the field.

His distressed team-mates said they weren't mentally fit to carry on and, in any case, playing here was clearly dangerous. The game had to be called off.

But there's no hiding place in the age of video and television. Pictures later showed that Rojas hadn't been hit by the firework at all. Yes, he did have a wound – but that had been self-inflicted, using a razor blade he'd hidden in his glove.

The goalkeeper was banned for life (although pardoned twelve years later), as was the team doctor Daniel Rodriguez and the coach, Orlando Aravena, who'd given instructions to the others via a walkie-talkie.

Chile were not only eliminated from the 1990 World Cup (the match was awarded to Brazil 2–0) but banned from the next one, too.

Match-fixing

There is, of course, a reason other than national glory for fixing the result of a football match – betting syndicates can make a fortune from it. You might reasonably imagine that no player found guilty of a crime so at odds with the spirit of the game could ever find his way onto a World Cup pitch afterwards, but that's not to allow for FIFA's own spirit of forgiveness. Here are three prodigal sons for whom it prepared the proverbial fatted calf:

• Luigi Allemandi

The great Italian defender played for Juventus, and in 1927 he took a bribe of 50,000 lire (half to be paid after the match) for helping his side lose to Torino in a title decider. Torino won 2–1, but Allemandi by all accounts played very well and he was refused the remaining 25,000 lire after the game. When the facts came to light Torino were stripped of the title and Allemandi was banned for life.

Pardoned by Prince Umberto of Savoy very soon afterwards, he was a member of Italy's World Cup squad in the Mussolini tournament of 1934, played in every match and picked up a winner's medal.

• Paolo Rossi

The 'golden boy' of Italian football played a part in the huge scandal which rocked his country's football in the early 1980s, with (among a wide dishing-out of punishments) Milan and Lazio being relegated to Serie B, other clubs being deducted points and several players and officials receiving bans.

The enemy within

When Italy were knocked out of the 2002 tournament by South Korea they blamed poor refereeing (and worse), and the players trashed their dressing room after the match.

What was particularly hard to take was the fact that the winning goal was scored by Ahn Jung-Hwan, who was playing on loan for Perugia in the Italian Serie A league.

Perugia's owner immediately announced that Ahn's time at the club was over. 'I have no intention,' he said, 'of paying a salary to someone who has ruined Italian football.'

Rossi was suspended for three years (later reduced to two on appeal) for taking a bribe before the match between Perugia and Avellino in December, 1979.

The smart money was on a 2–2 draw, which is exactly what happened, Rossi scoring both Perugia's goals. He later claimed that his reply to an Avellino player of '2–2? If you want!' was completely innocent.

Rossi was called up for the 1982 World Cup, although he hadn't had time to get himself properly match-fit, and he subsequently became the star of the tournament, won the Golden Boot for scoring most goals – and came away with a winner's medal.

• Eric Gerets

The bearded right back was Belgium's captain in the 1982 World Cup, and had also been the Standard Liège captain when they won the Belgian championship in the 1980–81 season. His powerful performances later won him a transfer to AC Milan, and it was while he was in Italy that the scandal broke.

1966

FACT FILE

- **Host country:** England.

- **Finalists:** Argentina, Brazil, Bulgaria, Chile, England, France, Hungary, Italy, Mexico, North Korea, Portugal, Spain, Switzerland, Uruguay, USSR, West Germany.

- **What happened:** Brazil now had an ageing team, which gave other countries hope – including England, manager Alf Ramsey's 'wingless wonders'.

  Scotland had been knocked out, with club managers in England refusing to release players for them. (Jock Stein resigned as manager because of this.)

  With FIFA president Stanley Rous telling referees to be lenient towards the 'virile' European kind of play, this was a rough World Cup, and Pelé – hacked in game after game until he could go on no longer – was among those who suffered .

- **Champions:** England.

- **What happened next:** Pelé, angry with the Brazilian team selection, vowed never to play in another World Cup – but fortunately later changed his mind.

It turned out that Standard (at the instigation of their president and their coach) had bribed the players of Waterschei in order to make sure that they won the league title. Gerets, who received a lengthy ban, was later given an amnesty – and, hey presto, up he popped to play for Belgium once again in both the 1986 and 1990 World Cup finals.

Ronaldo's time out

Had he been 'got at'? That was an early reaction to the strange case of the sleep-walking performance of Brazil's centre forward Ronaldo in the 1998 Final against France. But no: some sort of seizure rather than an artfully applied drug was the most common explanation for the fact that Ronaldo's name had first been taken off the team sheet; that it had then been reinstated at the last moment; and that he then lumbered about the pitch in a seeming daze during his side's 3-0 defeat. Had his sponsors Nike insisted that he play? No, said the coach. But why pick him then? It remains an unsolved mystery to this day.

A swig too far

What did Brazil's left back Branco swig from a 'water' bottle during a finals match against Argentina in June, 1990? And did it account for the fact that he then played the rest of the match in a drowsy state?

The weather in Turin was exhaustingly hot, but Branco was to claim that he'd been doped – and, much later, the then manager of Argentina, Carlos Bilardo, seemed to acknowledge that the bottle had, indeed, contained a tranquilliser.

Argentina, for the record, won the match 1–0.

Needle match

When this story surfaced, thoughts returned to the 1954 Final in Berne, when the much-fancied Hungarians went down to Germany. The suspicions then hadn't been about the losers being drugged but about the winners being pepped-up versions of their normal selves.

STATS CARD

Players receiving most cards:
6 Zinedine Zidane (France)
6 Cafu (Brazil)

Most sendings-off:
2 Rigobert Song (Cameroon)
2 Zinedine Zidane (France)

Sent off from the bench:
Claudio Caniggia, Argentina (v Sweden, 2002)

Most sendings-off all-time, teams:
11 Brazil

Most cautions all-time, teams:
88 Argentina

Most cautions in a single match:
9 Portugal (v Netherlands, 2006);
  Netherlands (v Spain, 2010)

Longest suspensions:
8 matches, Mauro Tassotti, Italy, 1994
  (elbowing an opponent)
1 year, Samir Shaker Mahmoud, Iraq, 1986
  (spitting at the referee)
15 months, Diego Maradona, Argentina,
  1994 (drugs)
Life (amnestied after 12 years), Roberto
  Rojas, Chile, 1989, for feigning injury
  from a firework

Puskas, the Hungarian captain, said he was suspicious when he saw several of the Germans vomiting in their dressing room after the game – and it was certainly strange that several of them went down with jaundice in the following weeks and took a long time to recover.

And then, fifty years after the event, a groundsman employed by the stadium revealed that he had come across several syringes there after the Final. A false memory? Well, no, because the doctor of the 1954 team, Franz Loogen, now stepped forward with an explanation. He had, he said, given his players vitamin C injections to enhance their stamina. The needles were dirty (hence the jaundice), because he'd had to use his old Soviet-style sterilisation heater which wasn't good enough to do a thorough job.

Three of the former players, now in their seventies, were sufficiently outraged to make a statement. The doctor, they claimed, had given them injections merely so that they would 'stay fresh'. It was, you might think, a strange sort of 'not guilty' plea.

Proof positive

Catching the drug-takers is a difficult business, but here are two cases that came to light during World Cup finals:

• **Willie Johnston, 1978**

You could say that luck didn't look kindly on the brilliant Scottish winger, because after losing 3–1 to Peru it was his team-mate Archie Gemmill who was asked to supply a urine sample. Gemmill was severely dehydrated, so Johnston took his place, and the test showed that he'd been using Fencamfamin pills. He was immediately sent home, banned from international football and told by the Scottish FA that he would never play for his country again.

• **Diego Maradona, 1994**

Here's a neat coincidence for you. When Argentina, captained by Maradona, beat Nigeria 2–1 in a first-round match, both their goals were scored by Claudio Caniggia, whose ban for cocaine use had conveniently run out just before the finals.

Bobby's dazzler

Was the trumped-up charge against England captain Bobby Moore in Colombia a ploy to unsettle the English squad before the 1970 finals in Mexico or simply a grubby attempt to fleece money from a visiting celebrity?

What happened was that Moore and team-mate Bobby Charlton came out of a jeweller's shop in Bogotá and were promptly questioned about a supposedly missing bracelet.

When the team returned to Colombia, having played against Ecuador in Quito, Moore was picked up by the police, put under house arrest and then bailed (after furious diplomatic negotiations, and with just five days to spare), so that he could take part in the World Cup.

Nobody in England considered for a moment that the decent, clean-living Moore could be guilty (it turned out to be a common scam in Bogotá, and its perpetrators were later charged with conspiracy), but the experience would have unsettled many another player.

In the event Moore went on to perform with even more impressive calm in Mexico than when leading England to World Cup victory four years before.

And Maradona? He'd already served a 15-month ban in Italy for cocaine offences but, apparently contrite, had returned to Buenos Aires, where he'd taken part in an official anti-drugs campaign.

Pure hypocrisy! He played the 90 minutes against Nigeria with enormous vigour, and soon everyone knew why. After the match a dope test revealed that his body contained no fewer than five variants of Ephedrine, a stimulant that enhances 'concentration and physical capacity'.

The Argentine FA immediately withdrew Maradona from the competition, but that didn't save him from another 15-month ban from FIFA, together with a small fine.

It was a sorry end to his professional playing career, but of course the world – and the World Cup – hadn't heard the last of the irrepressible Diego.

The underworld cup

The World Cup is such a vast money-spinning venture that it's open to all sorts of financial chicanery. A thorough judicial investigation after the 1990 tournament in Italy revealed that millions of lire had disappeared without trace in politically organised 'kick-backs'.

A new underground line was built in Rome – but it closed once the matches were over and has never been used since.

Luigi looked forward to taking everyone for a ride.

1970

- **Host country:** Mexico.

- **Finalists:** Belgium, Brazil, Bulgaria, Czechoslovakia, El Salvador, England, Israel, Italy, Mexico, Morocco, Peru, Sweden, Romania, Uruguay, USSR, West Germany.

FACT FILE

- **What happened:** This tournament, played in the intense heat of the Mexican day (some players were sent home with heat stroke), was the first in which red and yellow cards were used. It was also the first time that colour TV coverage of the finals was shown all around the world.

  Although England felt they had a good chance of retaining the cup, Brazil were the favourites, with Mario Zagallo newly appointed as their coach. They went on to win the tournament, playing sublime football and defeating Italy 4–1 in the Final.

- **Champions:** Brazil.

- **What happened next:** Brazil kept the Jules Rimet trophy, having won it for the third time. (it was later stolen.) This time Pelé really did retire for good.

Organised chaos

Mention it in a whisper, but some people think that FIFA itself is responsible for some of the problems with the World Cup. Here are a few of the gripes:

• TV schedules

The income from television being colossal, FIFA is obviously tempted to give the broacasters what they ask for – including live matches at the ideal time for their audiences. Mexico 1970 offers the worst example of this, with players having to play in exhausting, potentially dangerous heat so that European viewers could watch the games after coming home from work. It's a perennial problem.

• Stadiums

Any country staging the World Cup must of course be able to provide first-class facilities, but some of them have ended up with 'white elephant' stadiums at a great cost to their economies. That's their choice, but it sticks in the craw of poorer people who would rather the money was spent on life's essentials.

Evil spirits

When Haiti beat Trinidad 2–1 at home in a World Cup play-off before the 1974 finals their secret weapon was said to be the demonic power of voodoo.

How else can you explain the fact that Trinidad had no fewer than four goals disallowed?

Well, perhaps the touchline presence of the dictator 'Baby Doc' Duvalier and his armed thugs, the Tonton Macoutes, may have had some subtle influence, too.

Those who believed in the spirit world seemed to have their faith confirmed when the finals got under way. Haiti faced Italy, whose goalkeeper, Dino Zoff, had gone 1,097 minutes without conceding a goal in any competition before the match began – and yet they amazingly took the lead in the 46th minute.

Thereafter, unfortunately, someone must have plucked the pins out of the voodoo doll. Italy scored three times, and then Haiti went down to Poland 7–0 and Argentina 4–1.

• Tickets

This area is a minefield, with corruption, forgery and black-market sales a continuous danger. The allocation of tickets is also highly controversial, with FIFA giving large amounts to its major sponsors and other 'partners', with many more being set aside for 'corporate hospitality'. Ordinary fans, it's argued, are priced out in favour of important people who don't care very much about football at all.

• Sponsorship

Who benefits from it? FIFA chooses the main sponsors (huge multi-national companies), which means that the host nation has to find smaller backers – the crumbs from the rich man's table.

Trouble at the top

But all of this is nothing compared with the pitched battle which broke out at the very top of FIFA in 2002. The president, Sepp Blatter, was accused of serious misconduct by his own general secretary (and fellow Swiss), Michel Zen-Ruffinen, a qualified lawyer.

Zen-Ruffinen spoke about 'corruption through which one or two people had been bought', and he claimed that a 'look-alike impostor' had impersonated Haiti's delegate when Blatter was elected president four years earlier.

This followed hard on the heels of a call by UEFA president Lennart Johannson for an investigation into a report that a slush fund of $100 million had been set up in order to ensure Blatter's election.

Sunk by the *Titanic*

Sepp Blatter didn't always get things his own way – or not immediately. He wanted the 2006 finals to be played in South Africa, but the German satirical magazine *Titanic* scuppered that plan. It wrote hoax letters to FIFA representatives, offering gifts in exchange for a vote for Germany. It looked as though there would be a 12–12 tie between Germany and South Africa, with Blatter's vote swinging the decision his way. However, the Oceania delegate Charles Dempsey, who had been instructed to vote for South Africa, abstained at the last minute – citing 'intolerable pressure'.

With the president of the Somalian FA, Farah Ado, revealing that he'd been offered $100,000 for his vote, no fewer than eleven members of FIFA's executive committee now accused their president of corruption. Criminal proceedings seemed inevitable.

Beyond our Ken

The outspoken Chelsea chairman, Ken Bates (a man not unknown to controversy himself), wrote in the club's programme that he hoped the upcoming tournament in Japan and South Korea would be 'the last World Cup under the rotten, corrupt, crooked reign of Blatter'.

Surely he knew better than that!

At the FIFA congress a few days before the finals Blatter refused to let his opponents speak and was booed from the stage. A low point, you might think – but Blatter was re-elected president, the protesting committee members withdrew their complaint and Zen-Ruffinen was forced out.

Job done...

In December 2009 a poll conducted by *Sportbusiness International* magazine voted Blatter the most influential man in sport– and who could argue with that?

Four years later, after FIFA's ethics committee produced a devastating report about bribes paid to its officials, Blatter's predecessor João Havelange resigned 'for health and personal reasons' – but Blatter, despite having known about them, yet again emerged unscathed.

Who sets the rules?

When it comes to creating the laws of world football, the British punch above their weight.

The rules are fixed by the eight members of the International Football Association Board (IFAB), and any changes must be agreed by at least six of the eight delegates. FIFA has four representatives on the Board, and the other four are provided by the football associations of the United Kingdom (England, Scotland, Wales and Northern Ireland). This system was devised 'in recognition of their unique contribution to the creation and history of the game'.

Life and death

We end this chapter as we began it, with Bill Shankly's famous quote. A matter of life and death? It was exactly that for poor Andrés Escobar, who in the 1994 World Cup finals scored an own goal in Colombia's 2–1 defeat by the United States.

Colombia were eliminated and the team returned home. Two weeks later Escobar was approached outside the El Indio bar in a suburb of Medellín, the centre of the country's infamous drug cartels, and repeatedly shot – his killer, Humberto Muñoz, reportedly shouting 'Gol! Gol! Gol!' like some crazed commentator every time he pulled the trigger.

Escobar's funeral route was lined by 120,000 people and a statue was erected in his honour. Supporters, especially those of Atlético Nacional, continue to show their respect by taking photographs of him to matches. Muñoz, a schoolteacher, was sentenced to 43 years in jail for the murder, later reduced to 26 on appeal, but he was controversially released in 2005, having served only 11 years inside.

Money grabbing

You may think professional footballers earn ridiculous amounts of money, but that hasn't stopped them asking for more – not even when representing their countries in the World Cup.

The 1974 tournament in West Germany was a particularly hard-bargaining affair:

- A few days before the finals, players of the host nation threatened to pack their bags if they weren't offered winning bonuses to compare with those of the Dutch and Italian teams. After all-night talks (FIFA were warned that a second-string team might have to be brought in) the squad was still split 50–50 on whether to accept a revised offer. Franz Beckenbauer finally brokered a deal.

- Scotland's players, in a dispute with the kit manufacturer Adidas, decided to train with the company's logo blacked out with boot polish.

- Johan Cruyff, the Dutch captain, had a deal with Puma and therefore refused to wear the team strip with its three Adidas stripes. After negotiations he was allowed to play in a tailor-made kit with only two stripes.

- Uruguay's players refused to give any media interviews without payment – although, as they came bottom of their group, not many journalists wanted to talk to them anyway.

Why did he do it? It's not clear to this day whether it was simply an example of Latin American football enthusiasm at its over-the-top worst or an act of revenge on behalf of one of the local betting syndicates which had millions of dollars riding on Colombia advancing to the second round.

Certainly there had been trouble in the Colombian training camp well before the tournament began, with rumours circulating that the squad was being influenced by the powerful underworld of drugs and gambling. The coach, Hernán Gómez, was even reported to have received death threats over matters of team selection.

Coaches, after all, play a crucial role in World Cup football...

STATS CARD

World Cup champion coaches:

1930	Alberto Suppici, Uruguay
1934	Vittorio Pozzo, Italy
1938	Vittorio Pozzo, Italy
1950	Juan Lopez, Uruguay
1954	Sepp Herberger, Germany
1958	Vincente Feola, Brazil
1962	Aymore Moreira, Brazil
1966	Alf Ramsey, England
1970	Mario Zagallo, Brazil
1974	Helmut Schoen, Germany
1978	Cesar Luis Menotti, Argentina
1982	Enzo Bearzot, Italy
1986	Carlos Bilardo, Argentina
1990	Franz Beckenbauer, Germany
1994	Carlos Alberto Parreira, Brazil
1998	Aimé Jacquet, France
2002	Luiz Felipe Scolari, Brazil
2006	Marcello Lippi, Italy
2010	Vicente del Bosque, Spain

Most matches as coach:

25	Helmut Schoen, Germany
20	Mario Zagallo, Brazil
20	Bora Milutinovic, Yugoslavia
20	Carlos Alberto Parreira, Brazil
18	Sepp Herberger, Germany
18	Enzo Bearzot, Italy
18	Guus Hiddink, Holland

CHAPTER THREE

DUGOUT GENERALS

They're often an amusing pantomime spectacle on the touchline, those gesturing, growling, grimacing coaches and managers who display every emotion from joy to grief but can do nothing, when the going gets tough, except make a substitution and hope that it turns out to be inspired.

They *do* make a difference, of course, and they need every skill from man-management through technical nous to building a cohesive team, plus a large dose of stubborn self-belief when the critics gang up on them.

1974

- **Host country:** West Germany.

- **Finalists:** Argentina, Australia, Brazil, Bulgaria, Chile, East Germany, Haiti, Holland, Italy, Poland, Scotland, Sweden, Uruguay, West Germany, Yugoslavia, Zaire.

- **What happened:** There was another change in the way the finals were arranged. The top two teams from each group entered another league tournament, the top team in each group meeting in the Final.

  The Dutch brought with them a reputation for 'total football', with players swiftly interchanging at will.

  They began the Final by keeping possession for more than two minutes until a foul on Cruyff brought them a penalty from which they scored – but the Germans characteristically fought back to win 2–1.

- **Champions:** West Germany.

- **What happened next:** The German players' wives were banned from the post-match banquet. The players walked out, and Gerd Müller, the World Cup's top scorer, quit international football.

A club manager has the luxury of working with the same group of players week in, week out – often for years on end. The international manager, on the other hand, has to watch them from a distance, bringing a bunch of individuals together for intense preparation periods leading up to vital matches that can make or break his career overnight.

This chapter brings you thumbnail sketches of the men who have won the ultimate prize for their countries – aspiring coaches may pick up a few tips from the way they tackled the job.

Alberto Suppici (1930)

Uruguay's 'technical director', fondly known as The Professor, was luckier than most in that he was given his group of players for a full three months before the 1930 finals. This, don't forget, was a championship that his government very much wanted to win for propaganda purposes.

But he was also bold. When, just before the tournament began, his brilliant goalkeeper Andrés Mazali broke a curfew and failed to turn up at the team's hotel in time, Suppici instantly sent him home. His stand-in, Enrique Ballestrero, immediately kept two clean sheets, and the team went on to come from behind to beat Argentina in the Final.

Vittorio Pozzo (1934, 1938)

Here was another lucky man, you might say, in that Mussolini's iron fist gave him more control over his team, and lucky, additionally, that he was able to call on the 'oriundi' – players such as Luis Monti (page 68) who could claim some Italian blood in their veins and were now living in Italy. His reply to criticisms of this policy was no-nonsense: 'If they can die for Italy, they can also play for Italy.'

But Pozzo is the only man to have won the trophy back-to-back, and you need more than good fortune for that. Tactically, Pozzo developed the so-called 'metodo' formation recently introduced by Herbert Chapman of Arsenal and Hugo Meisl, the Austrian coach. This put more emphasis on attacking play, with a centre-half playing just behind the forwards and wingers who were expected to get on the score sheet more often. He later bolstered his defence in a 'sistema' 2–3–2–3 formation.

Was he himself a Fascist? The consensus is that he wasn't. He got his players to go through the motions 'because the Fascist flag is the official flag of the moment'. He ordered them to give the salute twice (page 40) for the sake of team morale.

Another doomed cup

We've heard about the tribulations of the Jules Rimet trophy, but at least it's probably still in one piece, wherever it's hidden.

In 1930 Vittorio Pozzo coached Italy to victory in the Central European International Cup, winning a fancy trophy made of Bohemian crystal. Unhappily, someone dropped it, and it broke into so many shards that it couldn't possibly be put together again. The victory mattered to Pozzo so much that he always carried a chip of the crystal in his pocket as a memorial.

He seems to have been a good psychologist too. Before the 1938 semi-final against Brazil in Marseille, he discovered that the Brazilians had booked the only plane flying the next day to Paris, where the Final was to be played.

STATS CARD

Most tournaments as coach:

6 Carlos Alberto Parreira
1982/90/94/98/2006/2010

5 Bora Milutinovic
1986/90/94/98/2002

4 Sepp Herberger
1938/54/58/62

4 Walter Winterbottom
1950/54/58/62

4 Helmut Schoen
1966/70/74/78

4 Lajos Baróti
1958/62/66/78

4 Henri Michel
1986/94/98/2006

When he asked if Italy could take over the booking should they win the match, he was apparently given the scoffing reply that there was no chance of that outcome – and he used this insult to fire up his players.

Juan Lopez (1950)

Uruguay's winning coach learned his trade at the feet of a master. Lopez was a medical assistant at a club in Montevideo managed by Alberto Suppici.

There's no record of his being a player of any note, but he picked up the fundamentals of coaching from Suppici and was in charge of the national team before he had turned forty.

Lopez was still in charge of the national team in 1954, when they reached the semi-final and took the brilliant Hungarians into extra time.

Sepp Herberger (1954)

This man is not only a footballing saint in Germany, but many credit him with being a founding father of the country's renewal after the Second World War. No, he wasn't a politician, a businessman or a great philanthropist – what he did was lead Germany to victory in their first post-war World Cup. That's power for you!

Herberger had been manager back in 1938, when the Germans had been knocked out early in the tournament. Now he was back to perform what his compatriots were to call 'the miracle of Berne'.

One thing he became known for was keeping a notebook containing the smallest details of his opponents' strengths and weaknesses. He was also fond of offering the world nuggets of footballing wisdom. Here are a few of them:

- The ball is round.
- A match lasts 90 minutes.
- The next game is always the toughest game.
- After the game is before the game.

⚽ 'football is a game of two... teams,' mused Herberger.

But you wouldn't argue the toss with him, because he was a tough authoritarian (the players all called him 'Chief') who knew his own mind.

After the Germans beat Turkey 4–1 in their opening game in Berne, Herberger rested several key players for their next one against the rampaging Hungarians. The Germans were duly slaughtered 8–3, and so, in the media, was Herberger.

But was he simply boxing clever? That was how it looked later, because Germany had to meet Turkey again in a play-off, and this time, with their best players suitably refreshed, they thrashed them 7–2.

In the Final, as we've seen, they met the Hungarians again, and beat them.

And his motivational skills? The captain, Fritz Walter, later recalled sitting next to him on the bus to the Final. 'It was raining so hard that the windscreen wipers were going at double speed. Herberger put his hand on my knee and said: "Your weather, Fritz."'

1978

- **Host country:** Argentina.

- **Finalists:** Argentina, Austria, Brazil, France, Holland, Hungary, Iran, Italy, Mexico, Peru, Poland, Scotland, Spain, Sweden, Tunisia, West Germany.

FACT FILE

- **What happened:** The finals took place in a country under the military dictatorship of General Jorge Videla. New stadiums were built for the tournament just in time, but the head of the body organising their completion was assassinated on his way to his first press conference.

  Holland, without Johan Cruyff, who had had enough of international football, reached the Final but went down 3–1 to the hosts in extra time.

- **Champions:** Argentina.

- **What happened next:** Argentina's captain, Daniel Passarella, received the trophy from the blood-stained hands of General Videla. Their coach, César Luis Menotti, prepared to unleash Diego Maradona on the next World Cup tournament.

Vincente Feola (1958)

In March 1958 the future FIFA president João Havelange took charge of the Brazilian football confederation and organised its complete overhaul.

Brazil had, by their own high standards, underperformed in the last two World Cups, and he decided that their approach had to be much more professional.

The portly Vincente Feola was appointed coach shortly before the finals, and found himself surrounded by an army of professional support, including a team manager, a doctor, a nutritionist and a psychologist.

Two future greats were in the party but weren't picked for the first two matches: Pelé, who was at first regarded as too young, and the brilliant winger Garrincha who was already setting crowds alight with his trickery.

Why no Garrincha? Because the psychologist thought he had a fatal flaw. He'd seen him playing against an Italian club team a few weeks before arriving in Sweden. Garrincha had dribbled through the entire defence, but then, instead of immediately scoring, had waited for one of his opponents to come back at him so that he could flick it round him again before putting the ball in the net. Unhinged!

Feola was apparently a good listener, and the other players knew what they wanted. The team wasn't in good shape, so Feola brought in Garrincha and the 17-year-old Pelé – and they won the rest of their games.

Aymore Moreira (1962)

There's not much to be said about him except that he was the brother of Zeze, who had managed Brazil in 1954 – oh, and that he won the cup for them again in 1962 despite having an ageing team and an injured Pelé, who couldn't finish the tournament. Not bad going.

Alf Ramsey (1966)

A strange man, who tried to hide a working-class upbringing behind a 'proper' accent, who had an aloof manner and therefore a difficult relationship with the media, and yet who earned the unquestioning respect of his players, Ramsey did the impossible – he won the World Cup for England.

Not that *he* thought it impossible: very early on he said he would, 'without a doubt'. And there was good reason to believe him. After all, he'd taken an unfashionable club, Ipswich, all the way up from the basement of the English leagues to win the Division I (today's Premiership) title – in just a few seasons and with very limited talent at his disposal.

When he became England's manager he demanded full control over the squad selection, something that (incredibly, it now seems) his predecessor Walter Winterbottom never had. He picked teams for particular occasions, and he dispensed with wingers when he found he didn't have any good enough for the job.

He was shrewd, too. When Germany scored a late equaliser in the Final, Ramsey was swiftly on the pitch at the final whistle before extra time to make sure that his players didn't flop out on the ground in their exhaustion – that, he reasoned, would give the Germans a psychological advantage. Instead he urged them on: 'You've won the match once: now go out and win it again!'

STATS CARD

Coached more than three countries:

5 **Bora Milutinovic** (Yugoslavia)
1986 Mexico; 1990 Costa Rica;
1994 (USA); 1998 Nigeria; 2002 China.

5 **Carlos Alberto Parreira** (Brazil)
1982 Kuwait; 1990 United Arab Emirates;
1994/2006 Brazil; 1998 Saudi Arabia;
2010 South Africa.

4 **Henri Michel** (France)
1986 France; 1994 Cameroon;
1998 Morocco; 2006 Ivory Coast.

Mario Zagallo (1970)

Brazil won all six of their matches in the 1970 tournament, and Zagallo's genius was to use a flexible 5–3–2 formation that could best use the talents of a remarkable squad including Pelé, Jairzinho, Tostao, Gerson and Rivelino. Known as 'The Professor', he was notoriously susperstitious about the number 13. He pointed out that the years 1958 (when he scored in the Final) and 1994 (we're getting ahead of

That 'Russian' linesman

Did Geoff Hurst's first extra-time goal in the 4–2 victory over Germany in 1966 really cross the line? The phrase 'Russian linesman' is always repeated with a smile in England when there's a touch-and-go decision – although the 'lino' who told the referee that the ball HAD bounced down from the bar over the goal-line was actually an Azerbaijani, Tofik Bakhramov.

They loved the publicity in Baku, Azerbaijan's capital, and still do. The national stadium is named after him, and there's a statue to him outside. It was unveiled with several footballing VIPs in attendance – including Geoff Hurst.

ourselves here) must be lucky, because $5+8$ and $9+4$ both equal 13. And, he'd ask for good measure, how many letters are there in the phrase 'Brasil Campeão'?

Helmut Schoen (1974)

He worked long and hard for his World Cup success, did Schoen. Deputy to Sepp Herberger, he took over the national team for the 1966 World Cup and led it in three more tournaments thereafter. His triumph came in 1974, when he became the oldest coach at that time to win the trophy.

César Luis Menotti (1978)

Staying cool under pressure is a useful ability in a football manager, and Menotti needed to play his familiar role of Mr Suave like a trouper when he coached the Argentina team on home soil in 1978. The atmosphere in Buenos Aires was electric. On the political front, the country was being run by a cruel dictatorship receiving a terrible press all around the world. On the football front, the fans were desperate for success, having played second fiddle to the Brazilians for years.

Menotti's politics were to the left of centre. He wore his hair long, dressed casually, chain-smoked and dropped the names of writers and singers. No doubt he calculated that the politicians needed him more than he needed them: a few years later, under another repressive regime, he would make critical remarks about military rule, and President Galtieri (pages 61–62) would come to the training camp and hug him in front of the cameras.

For 1978 he had to cope with the withdrawal of top players by the Boca Juniors and River Plate clubs, and he thought it was too early to introduce Diego Maradona to the World Cup. Many Argentine players had moved to Spain since the previous tournament, and Menotti was disinclined to bring them back. He made an exception of centre forward Mario Kempes, however, and that proved crucial.

He scored twice as Argentina beat Holland 3–1 in the Final, and Menotti was the hero of the hour.

1982

FACT FILE

- **Host country:** Spain.

- **Finalists:** Algeria, Argentina, Austria, Belgium, Brazil, Cameroon, Chile, Czechoslovakia, El Salvador, England, France, Honduras, Hungary, Italy, Kuwait, New Zealand, Northern Ireland, Peru, Poland, Scotland, Spain, USSR, West Germany, Yugoslavia.

- **What happened:** FIFA increased the number of finalists to 24, with an increased participation from Africa, Asia and Central America.

  Diego Maradona made his first appearance in the finals (and would be sent off), while Italy's Paolo Rossi came back from a match-fixing scandal to be the star of the tournament.

- **Champions:** Italy.

- **What happened next:** Brazil applied to stage the 1986 tournament, but FIFA's president, the Brazilian João Havelange, had had a serious falling-out with the president of the Brazilian Football Federation and therefore opposed its being held in his own country. He prevailed.

1986

- **Host country:** Mexico.

- **Finalists:** Algeria, Argentina, Belgium, Brazil, Bulgaria, Canada, Denmark, England, France, Hungary, Iraq, Italy, Mexico, Morocco, Northern Ireland, Paraguay, Poland, Portugal, Scotland, South Korea, Spain, Uruguay, USSR, West Germany.

- **What happened:** Why did Mexico host again and not the USA, which had also put in a bid? There was outrage when it was announced that the tournament would be staged by the Mexican TV company Televisa, one of whose executives was a close friend of FIFA's president, João Havelange. Camel cigarettes were a major sponsor.

  There were 24 finalists again, but the second-stage mini-leagues were replaced by a knock-out competition. Penalty shoot-outs were introduced to settle games that had gone to extra time.

- **Champions:** Argentina.

- **What happened next:** The so-called Mexican Wave became a supporters' ritual at stadiums around the world.

Enzo Bearzot (1982)

Italy got off to a dreadful start in 1982, with three draws in a row, and Bearzot's reaction was to announce a 'silenzio stampa' or media silence. (He wouldn't be able to get away with that today.) They went on to play brilliantly, with Rossi – the coach's trump card – scoring freely.

Bearzot, who usually had a pipe dangling out of his mouth, was a greatly loved coach who always insisted that the game should be enjoyed.

'For me, coaching Italy was a vocation,' he said when he eventually stepped down, adding that it had since become a profession.

'The game's values have changed since my day. Due to the development of football and the arrival of powerful sponsors, it seems as if money has moved all the goalposts.'

Carlos Bilardo (1986)

A doctor by training and a tough left-half on the football field, Bilardo brought a down-to-earth attitude to winning the World Cup for Argentina. He had no decent strikers or wingers to call on, he said, so he was forced to play with a sweeper, a packed midfield and one man alone up front. The president of the country publicly criticised him, but Bilardo in effect told him to 'lump it'. He had a job to do. What he *did* have, of course, was Diego Maradona – and that was enough.

Franz Beckenbauer (1990)

We'll meet him shortly with the ball at his feet, but the German sweeper is one of only two men – Brazil's Zagallo was the other – to have won the World Cup as a player (1974) and a manager (1990). He's a great example of the power of personality in management. Appointed despite having none of the coaching qualifications the Germans normally demand, he inspired his teams to two consecutive Finals, and they won the second of them.

Carlos Alberto Parreira (1994)

South Africa's manager for the 2010 finals, Parreira started badly as Brazil's coach ahead of the 1994 tournament. In Ecuador they suffered defeat in a qualifying match for the first time in their history, and they had to beat Uruguay in order to go through.

This is when Parreira swallowed his pride. He'd received a lot of stick for playing a 'European' type of football – which meant defensive, rather than with flair – and he'd left out the scintillating forward Romario, with whom he'd had a bit of a spat in the past. In 1994 he called him back, and was rewarded with a brace of goals from the striker and an essential victory.

STATS CARD

Youngest coach:
Juan José Tramutola, Argentina (1930)
27 years, 267 days

Oldest coach:
Otto Rehhagel, Greece (2010)
71 years, 317 days

Brazil reached the Final against Italy, and Parreira had the players walk out onto the pitch holding hands in a gesture of solidarity. He'd feared the skill of the Italians.

'It was like a chess game,' he said later. 'The one who moves the wrong piece loses the World Cup.' It was a fairly tedious chess game, played by two cagey opponents, and it ended in a stalemate, with Brazil winning on penalties.

Aimé Jacquet (1998)

Patience was the key for France's Jacquet. Like Parreira before him, he was strongly criticised before the 1998 tournament for his team's defensive play, which the media called 'palaeolithic', and there were cries of 'resign!' when, in the year before the finals, France finished a tournament below Brazil, England and Italy.

It didn't help that he goofed in drawing up his list of players in the month before the finals – he was supposed to name a squad of 22 players, but chose 28. The sports daily

L'Équipe declared that he wasn't the man for the job. But timing is all. When the competition began the team were in good heart, and they hammered Brazil 3–0 in the Final.

Luiz Felipe Scolari (2002)

'Big Phil', as the British press liked to call him during a brief spell managing Chelsea, is the kind of colourful character who wears his heart on his sleeve and demands absolute control over his teams.

His volatile temperament (he once swung a punch at a Serbian defender while managing Portugal in a European match) perhaps explains the gift he gave each of his Brazilian players at the 2002 finals in Japan and South Korea – Sun Tzu's *The Art of War*, a military treatise written during the 6th century BC.

Here was another case of a manager braving the storm. Brazil just squeezed into the finals, but they won every game when they got there. And then the warlord resigned, triumphant.

'Big Phil' Scolari liked to
instil a love of literature
in his players.

Marcello Lippi (2006)

If the personable Lippi had given his Italy players a book for bedtime reading in 2006 it could have been his own, because he outlined his philosophy of coaching in *Il Gioco delle Idee: Pensieri e Passioni da Bordo Campo* ('The Play of Ideas: Thoughts and Passions from the Touchline.')

His achievement in winning the World Cup was the more remarkable in that his players couldn't help but be affected by the so-called Moggiopoli match-fixing scandal which had recently rocked Serie A. Phone-tapping had revealed widespread deals between team managers and referee organisations, and the outcome was relegation to Serie B for Juventus, points reduction for them and other top clubs such as AC Milan, Fiorentina, Lazio and Reggina, and a swathe of fines and bans.

Just before the quarter-final against Ukraine the players heard that the Juventus general manager had thrown himself from a window at the club's headquarters in Turin. There were five Juventus players in the squad, and two of them flew home to visit their friend in intensive care. Somehow Lippi steered his squad through all this to win the trophy. He resigned immediately afterwards, but when Italy were knocked out of the European championships in 2008 he was reappointed for the next World Cup campaign in South Africa.

And that philosophy of his? It included the thought that putting together the best *blend* of players is more important than simply choosing the best player for each position.

True, no doubt – but when it comes to the World Cup it's the most exciting players that the fans want to see...

CHAPTER FOUR

STAR QUALITY

Never mind the political shenanigans, the fouls, the match-fixing, the drugs and all the rest of it – as soon as another World Cup arrives those of us who love our football thrust cynicism aside and hope against hope for a new flowering of what Danny Blanchflower called 'the glory game'.

And never mind the clever tactics and the battle formations dreamed up by canny coaches – what most of us want to see is creative players doing scintillating things with the ball. That's what this chapter is about.

The best goal ever?

The great goals come in all forms, from sensational long-distance net-breakers to individual feats of dribbling brilliance, but it was the teamwork and the occasion rather than the finish itself that made Carlos Alberto's goal for Brazil in the 1970 Final against Italy so outstanding.

It's four minutes from the end. Brazil, 3–1 up and cruising, are not only about to be crowned champions but have enthralled spectators throughout the tournament with breathtaking sambas of vivacious attacking football and a flurry of wonderful goals. Can they put the icing on the cake?

They do. The move begins deep in their own half and ripples man to man in pretty patterns across the pitch. Clodoaldo feeds Jairzinho – who has scored in every match these finals – and he switches the ball to the incomparable Pelé who has arrived inside the penalty area.

How does he know that his full-back and captain is arriving at pace to his right? Without looking up, he turns and squares the ball into the path of the flying Alberto – who drills it unerringly into the far corner.

Very soon the final whistle blows and the yellow Brazilian shirts come off in celebration under the Mexican sun. Who can ever forget?

Here are ten of the most exciting players from post-war World Cup tournaments. Included is no more than one star per country. This means, for example, that the rich crop of Brazilian maestros over the years has to be represented by a single individual – and there are no marks for guessing who *he* may be.

Defenders, alas, don't get much of a look-in, great as many of them have been. We're looking for players who lift the spirits.

1 Pelé

Of course! Skill, strength, speed and athleticism are just a few attributes of a player who burst onto the world scene as a lad of 17 and made an immediate impact.

Here's your literal rags-to-riches story. Born into poverty as Edson Arantes do Nascimento (well, wouldn't you change *your* name if it was a mouthful like that?), Pelé first played his football in the streets of São Paulo, kicking stockings packed with rags and paper because he and his mates couldn't afford a ball.

A slouch at school, he was electric once he stepped onto a football pitch – devastating both on the ground and in the air. He signed for the Santos club, went into the first team at the age of 16 and promptly scored 36 goals in 29 matches. The following season this became 58 in 38, and he joined the national squad.

He first stepped onto the World Cup stage in a first-round match in Sweden in 1958. In the next game, a quarter-final tie, he scored the only goal in a 1–0 victory over Wales. He then notched a hat-trick in the semi-final against France and another two in the Final, when Brazil beat the hosts 5–2. Pelé had arrived.

Injuries prevented him finishing the next two tournaments, but in the 1970 finals in Mexico he was part of a dazzling forward line (with Jairzinho, Gérson, Tostão and Rivelino) who ran their opponents ragged and won the cup in rampaging style.

In the twilight of his career he played for New York Cosmos, raising the profile of the game in the USA, and he's since assumed the role of special ambassador for football.

2 Diego Maradona

If Maradona runs Pelé close as a player, he's certainly nobody's idea of a suave diplomat. Like Northern Ireland's George Best (not included here, since he never appeared in the World Cup finals), he poisoned his body and paid a heavy price.

With Best it was alcohol. With Maradona it was drugs, and the amazing thing is that he bounced back as often as he did.

Even his greatest moment of glory – the winning of the World Cup for Argentina in 1986 – was marred by the infamous 'hand of God' incident.

Peter Shilton never had a prayer.

STATS CARD

FIFA World Cup all-time rankings:

	P	W	D	L	GF	GA	Pts	Ave
1 BRAZIL	97	67	15	15	210	88	216	2.23
2 GERMANY	99	60	19	20	206	117	199	2.017
3 ITALY	80	44	21	15	126	74	153	1.917
4 ARGENTINA	70	37	13	20	123	80	124	1.77
5 ENGLAND	59	26	19	14	77	52	97	1.64
6 SPAIN	56	28	12	16	88	59	96	1.71
7 FRANCE	54	25	11	18	96	68	86	1.59
8 NETHERLANDS	43	22	10	11	71	44	76	1.77
9 URUGUAY	47	18	12	17	76	65	66	1.40
10 SWEDEN	46	16	13	17	74	69	61	1.33

In the quarter-finals he punched the ball past England's goalkeeper Peter Shilton for the opening goal, later saying it had been scored 'a little with the head of Maradona and a little with the hand of God'.

A callous cheat, therefore – but what strength and balance, and what wonderful dribbling skills! Four minutes after that calamity, England were struck down by a mazy run which left four defenders and Shilton in his wake.

Many forget that he produced a near-carbon-copy goal against Belgium in the semi-finals before lifting the cup as captain after West Germany were defeated in the Final.

Despite having two bans for drug-taking, Maradona came back to manage the national team. A reformed character? *Don't be silly!*

After Argentina only scraped through to the 2010 finals in a tense 1–0 victory over Uruguay, Maradona directed a foul-mouthed rant at the media who had criticised him – and was 'handed' a two-month ban by FIFA.

The tears of a clown

Paul 'Gazza' Gascoigne might have become one of the great ball-players of the English game had his personal demons not damaged his career. He was always emotionally close to the edge, and the photograph of him in tears during the 1990 World Cup became a footballing icon.

A few minutes before the end of the semi-final with West Germany, Gazza picked up a booking which meant he would miss the Final should England get through. (In the event they lost on penalties.)

The tears won him huge publicity, but the foul which preceeded them had been a completely unnecessary tackle out by the touchline. As the England manager Bobby Robson put it, Gazza was 'daft as a brush'.

Gazza cried all the way to the bank.

3 Ferenc Puskas

The Hungarian inside forward didn't look at all dangerous, being on the short side and tending to plumpness as he got older, but he had brilliant control and the best left foot in the business.

He was the creative genius of the team (arguably the best not to have won the World Cup) which in 1953 revealed what years of complacency had done to English football. Hungary won 6–3 at Wembley and then, six months later, thrashed England 7–1 at home.

They arrived at the 1954 finals in Switzerland with the record of having been undefeated for four years. Puskas scored in the Final despite being injured, but Hungary narrowly lost.

After the Soviet invasion of Hungary (page 47), Puskas joined Real Madrid, where he formed a prolific partnership with the wonderful Alfredo di Stefano – like Best, not included here because he never took part in the World Cup finals.

✝ Franz Beckenbauer

They called him the Kaiser because of the way he marshalled and inspired his teams, but Beckenbauer's supreme grace and coolness under pressure seemed to raise him above the skirmish of battle all around him.

He first saw World Cup action in 1966 as an elegant right-half, when Germany reached the Final and lost to England. By the time his country hosted the tournament in 1974 he had revamped the 'libero' role introduced by the Italians in the 1960s – a free man who mopped up behind a massed defence – to make the sweeper a creative force, swiftly switching the impetus from defence to attack.

Beckenbauer, always a natural leader, was captain of Germany when they won the cup that year. Drawn away by the lure of dollars to join Pelé at the Cosmos, he eventually came back as manager, taking Germany to two successive World Cup finals – and when they won it in 1990, he became the first player to lift the trophy as both captain and manager.

1990

- **Host country:** Italy.

- **Finalists:** Argentina, Austria, Belgium, Brazil, Cameroon, Colombia, Costa Rica, Czechoslovakia, Egypt, England, Holland, Italy, Republic of Ireland, Romania, Scotland, South Korea, Sweden, Spain, United Arab Republic, Uruguay, USA, USSR, West Germany, Yugoslavia.

- **What happened:** This was one of the dullest, most negative tournaments in World Cup history, with very few goals scored.

  West Germany were the first team to keep a clean sheet in the Final (they beat Argentina 1–0), and scored only a single goal in each of their last three matches.

- **Champions:** West Germany.

- **What happened next:** Because the finals were so poor, FIFA considered several extreme suggestions for improving the game, such as making the goals larger. A change that *was* agreed was a ban on goalkeepers picking up back passes.

1994

- **Host country:** USA.

- **Finalists:** Argentina, Belgium, Bolivia, Brazil, Bulgaria, Cameroon, Colombia, Germany, Greece, Holland, Italy, Mexico, Morocco, Nigeria, Norway, Republic of Ireland, Romania, Russia, Saudi Arabia, South Korea, Spain, Sweden, Switzerland, USA.

- **What happened:** The USA put on a highly professional tournament, although the playing of indoor matches in the heat of the summer was unpopular.

  FIFA president João Havelange banned Pelé from the opening ceremony because he had criticised the head of the Brazilian FA – who was Havelange's brother-in-law.

  Argentina, with the 33-year-old Maradona as captain, were the favourites, but he tested positive for drugs and they went out.

- **Champions:** Brazil.

- **What happened next:** Colombia's Escobar, who had scored an own goal early in the tournament, was shot dead shortly after his return home.

5 Johan Cruyff

Not many players have a football manoeuvre named after them. The 'Cruyff turn' involves feinting to cross and instead slipping the ball behind your standing leg to bamboozle an opponent – something the Dutchman first used against Sweden in the 1974 World Cup. (Mind you, an acceleration like Cruyff's also comes in handy in order to escape before the defender realises what you've done to him.)

Cruyff, an attacking midfielder who scored 33 goals in 48 internationals, was part of the tactically advanced Holland team which preached and played 'total football'.

He epitomised the fluidity demanded by the system, often starting as a centre forward, but dropping deep or switching to the wings in a bid to outwit his markers.

In Cruyff's philosophy the ball was something to be held and nursed – by individuals and by the team as a whole. Mindless hoofing was for the barbarians.

Not surprisingly, Cruyff also made a great coach, first with Ajax in his own country and then with Barcelona, whose 'dream team' won the 1992 European Cup and four league titles in a row.

6 Michel Platini

French flair is what comes to mind. Probably the best attacking midfielder ever to play for his country, Platini had the misfortune to orchestrate a team good enough for European success but not to win the world crown.

His first finals, when he was 21, were in Argentina in 1978, and France, although playing good football, went out early. Four

STATS CARD

All-time top goalscorers:
15 Ronaldo (Brazil)
14 Gerd Muller (Germany)
13 Just Fontaine (France)
12 Pelé (Brazil)
11 Jurgen Klinsmann (Germany)
11 Sándor Kocsis (Hungary)

years later, with Platini established as captain, they reached the semi-finals, losing to two late West Germany goals in 'the Battiston match' (page 81). Another four years on and, with Platini not fully fit, they went out to the Germans at the semi-final stage – and that was the end of Platini's World Cup adventure.

Playing for Juventus in Serie A, he picked up the European Player of the Year award in 1983, 1984 and 1985 (the first since Cruyff to pick it up three times in a row).

Platini's special skills were the deft passes he could contrive out of nothing and an astonishing success with free kicks at a time when there were far fewer specialists of the art than there are today. This wasn't pure innate skill: he used to practise on the training ground with rows of dummies deployed in front of the goal.

After retiring, he coached an attractive but not highly successful France team for four years and then went into football administration. He became president of the Union of European Football Associations (UEFA) in 2007.

World Cup classics

For a game to be regarded as great it arguably has to be played with great skill and power between two well-matched teams at a crucial moment in the tournament. Here are three such epics which have become legendary:

Hungary 4 – Uruguay 2
30 June 1954, Lausanne, Switzerland
This semi-final thriller pitted the vibrant Hungarian team of Grosics, Kocsis, Hidegkuti and Czibor (although not Puskas, who was injured) against the World Cup holders (without their own captain Obdulio Varela).

Hungary were two up by the 47th minute, but the skilful South Americans came right back into it with a brace from their naturalised Argentinian Juan Eduardo Hohberg. The equaliser came with only three minutes left – and Hohberg was knocked out by his own team-mates in the celebration.

He recovered to hit a post early in extra time, and that left Kocsis – a man with an incredibly muscular neck – to settle things with two powerful headers.

Hungary's manager said they'd just beaten the best team they had ever played against.

Italy 4 – West Germany 3
17 June 1970, Mexico City, Mexico
Another semi-final epic which went into extra time, this match swung back and forth in breath-taking fashion.

Italy drew first blood with an 8th-minute goal from Boninsegna, and it wasn't until the third minute of injury time that Schnellinger made a two-footed leap to a cross by Grabowski and volleyed home the equaliser.

The goals came thick and fast after that in the blazing Mexican sun. Müller put Germany ahead for the first time just four minutes after the re-start, but Burgnich equalised and Luigi Riva restored Italy's lead just before the break.

Beckenbauer was by now a passenger, with his arm in a sling, but the Germans battled back with another Müller goal on 104 minutes. It wasn't enough: Gianni Rivera completed the scoring a minute later, calmly side-footing in a low cross.

It was a coach's nightmare; a fan's delight.

Italy 3 – Brazil 2
5 July 1982, Barcelona, Spain
Brazil needed only a draw to advance from the second round to the semi-finals, but a hat-trick from Paolo Rossi finally sank them.

Italy led within five minutes, but were soon pegged back by the Brazilian captain, Socrates. Rossi's second came on 25 minutes and another 43 minutes had passed before Falcão struck a forceful equaliser and ran round the pitch with his contorted face the picture of delight.

Then Rossi swivelled and shot for his third, the 40-year-old Dino Zoff made an athletic save from Oscar on his goal-line – and Italy had taken another step on their way to winning the World Cup.

1998

- **Host country:** France.

- **Finalists:** Argentina, Austria, Belgium, Brazil, Bulgaria, Cameroon, Chile, Colombia, Croatia, Denmark, England, France, Germany, Holland, Iran, Italy, Jamaica, Japan, Mexico, Morocco, Nigeria, Norway, Paraguay, Romania, Saudi Arabia, Scotland, South Africa, South Korea, Spain, Tunisia, USA, Yugoslavia.

- **What happened:** The number of competing teams was increased to 32, with eight groups of four in mini-leagues followed by a succession of knock-out rounds.

  A new 'golden goal' rule was introduced for the second round. The tackle from behind was banned, and for the first time boards were held up to show how much time was left at the end of a game.

  The Final between France and Brazil was marred by Ronaldo's 'sleep-walking' condition (page 92).

- **Champions:** France.

- **What happened next:** Sepp Blatter took over as FIFA president.

7 Eusébio

The Mozambique-born player was a strong and incredibly fast attacker with a huge, engaging smile that won him fans across the world.

His goal-scoring was prolific (an amazing 727 goals in 715 games for Benfica) and it was crucial in taking Portugal to the 1966 World Cup semi-finals: he notched a tally of nine in just six matches.

His most dramatic performance was in the quarter-final match against North Korea – a lightweight team who had managed to dispose of Italy but were thought to be inferior opponents. That's not how it looked as they scored in just 55 seconds and went 3–0 up within 24 minutes. The crowd simply couldn't believe their eyes.

But Eusébio had been in exceptional form, and now he began to impose himself with strong running and lethal shooting. By the 60th minute he had struck four times, twice from penalties, and Portugal eventually ran out 5–3 winners. The fifth goal, perhaps it should be added, came from a Eusébio corner.

Playing in a national team not quite good enough to win a trophy (they took third spot that year), he picked up his cups and medals with Benfica – no fewer than eleven Portuguese league titles and the European Cup in 1962. He scored twice in that final.

8 Paolo Maldini

When he picked up his 'World player of the year' award from *World Soccer* magazine in 1994, Maldini said it was 'a particular matter of pride because defenders generally receive so much less attention from fans and the media than goalscorers'.

That's true of this list, too, but how can you argue with the credentials of a man who won a shoal of cups and championships with AC Milan, represented his country in no fewer than four World Cups and was captain in the last three of them, from 1994 to 2002?

In 2009, as he prepared to play his 900th game for Milan, the striker Allesandro Del Piero described him as 'quite simply the best there is,' while Manchester United's manager, Alex Ferguson, has named him as his favourite player among all his opponents over the years.

The sad thing for Maldini is that, although he wore the captain's armband a record 74 times, this was a barren period for Italy, and they didn't pick up a single trophy.

Milla's tail

Unbridled joy is the goalscorer's privilege, especially in the World Cup finals – and few have expressed it better than Roger Milla of Cameroon.

At the age of 38 he became a star of the 1990 tournament, when Cameroon were the first African side to reach the quarter-finals, repeatedly coming on as a 'super sub' to make and score goals. Back again in 1994, he became the oldest player to score a goal in the finals.

His trademark celebration was a run to the corner flag, a wiggle of his hips and a shake of his bottom. Happiness!

The Maldini family runs through AC Milan like lettering in a stick of rock. Paolo's centre-half father, Cesare, was the club's captain before him, and he also coached the Italy team in the 1998 finals, with his son leading the side. Milan thought so highly of Paolo that they paid him an incredible compliment when he left – they 'retired' their no. 3 shirt, reserving it for either of his two sons should either make the grade and step up from the youth side to the first team.

The greatest ever save?

The first-round game between Brazil and England in 1970 matched two of the favourites and produced a thrilling game. It was also notable for what has gone down as one of the greatest World Cup saves of all time.

With ten minutes gone, Jairzinho escaped down the right and centred perfectly for Pelé, whose bullet header from an athletic leap was so obviously bound for the bottom corner of the net that Brazilian fans were already on their feet when the impossible happened – goalkeeper Gordon Banks threw himself to his right and, with one fist, lifted the ball over the bar.

The *left back* was *all* too aware of Maldini's *legacy*.

Unusually for a modern football star, Maldini managed to keep his private affairs out of the public glare. Not much was known about his life away from the pitch other than that he was married to his childhood sweetheart – and owned more than a hundred pairs of jeans.

9 Henrik Larsson

The case *against* Swede Larsson's inclusion will probably focus on the fact that this speedy and skilful striker played most of his league football against lesser opposition in Sweden and then with Celtic in Scotland.

And of course he never won World Cup glory. He first appeared (with blond dreadlocks rather than the shaven head which became his trademark) at the 1994 tournament in the USA, when he started a match only in the third-place final and scored in Sweden's 4–0 victory over Bulgaria.

He was a regular in 2002 – the next time that they reached the finals – scoring both goals in a win over Nigeria and the only goal when

2002

FACT FILE

- **Host countries:** Japan and South Korea.

- **Finalists:** Argentina, Belgium, Brazil, Cameroon, China, Costa Rica, Croatia, Denmark, Ecuador, England, France, Germany, Italy, Japan, Mexico, Nigeria, Paraguay, Poland, Portugal, Republic of Ireland, Russia, Saudi Arabia, Senegal, Slovenia, South Africa, South Korea, Spain, Sweden, Tunisia, Turkey, Uruguay, USA.

- **What happened:** The first World Cup to be held in Asia, it was preceded by a record 777 qualifying matches.

  Argentina and France were the favourites, but Brazil beat Germany in the Final, with two Ronaldo goals.

- **Champions:** Brazil.

- **What happened next:** After a goal from South Korea's Perugia player Ahn knocked Italy out of the tournament, Perugia's owner said he would tear up Ahn's contract for ruining Italian football. Many Italians blamed the Ecuadorian referee for their defeat – and a row of toilets was named after him at a holiday resort in Sicily.

2006

- **Host country:** Germany.

- **Finalists:** Angola, Argentina, Australia, Brazil, Costa Rica, Croatia, Czech Republic, Ecuador, England, France, Germany, Ghana, Holland, Iran, Italy, Ivory Coast, Japan, Mexico, Paraguay, Poland, Portugal, Saudi Arabia, Serbia and Montenegro, South Korea, Spain, Sweden, Switzerland, Togo, Trinidad and Tobago, Tunisia, Ukraine, USA.

- **What happened:** The tournament came back to Germany for the frst time since their victory in 1974, and they had a dynamic new coach in Jürgen Klinsmann.

  The French, with an ageing team, started poorly, and Italy might have been expected to be affected by a match-fixing scandal at home, but these two teams reached the Final, with Italy winning on penalties after Zidane was sent off for a head-butt.

- **Champions:** Italy.

- **What happened next:** Zidane picked up the Golden Ball as the tournament's best player – and then retired from the game.

Sweden went out to Senegal. Immediately after the match he announced his retirement from international football.

The case *for* is that he scored 242 goals in seven seasons for Celtic, becoming a club legend, and then moved to Barcelona where, despite being in his mid-thirties, he scored ten goals during the 2005–6 season in which they won the Spanish title.

This is what Ronaldinho said about him: 'Henrik was my idol and now that I am playing next to him it is fantastic.'

And Thierry Henry was equally effusive after Larrson came on as a substitute in the Champions League final against Arsenal (his last game for Barcelona) and turned the match from 0–1 to a 2–1 victory with two assists.

'You talk about Ronaldinho and Eto'o and people like that,' he said. 'You need to talk about the proper footballer who made the difference, and that was Henrik Larsson.'

We rest our case.

10 David Beckham

No, we're not claiming a place among the footballing greats for the English midfielder, but don't forget the title of this chapter. When it comes to star quality – which in his case means international celebrity – nobody better epitomises the glamour of the sport in the twenty-first century.

Beckham's skills were genuine but limited. He could pass a 40-yard ball with inch-perfect precision, and he was one of the best free-kick specialists in the business: it was his shot round the defensive wall which won his country a last-minute World Cup qualification against Greece in 2001.

STATS CARD

Youngest goalscorer:
Pelé 17 years, 239 days,
Brazil v Wales 1958

Oldest goalscorer:
Roger Milla 42 years, 39 days,
Cameroon v Russia 1994

Set against this were a lack of pace, doubtful tackling skills and an inability to take the ball past his man – and that's without raising the problem of his temperament.

But let's raise it anyway. After being barged over by Diego Simeone in the 1998 World Cup finals, Beckham – lying on the ground – stupidly waved a leg in his direction. The Argentine captain predictably collapsed and the referee produced a red card. England went out on penalties.

A rare lapse? Hardly: during his time at Real Madrid, from 2003 to 2007, he picked up 41 yellow cards and four reds. But that's not the point about David Beckham. Here are a *few* points about him:

- He's very good-looking, if you like that kind of thing.
- He's married to the former Spice Girl Victoria Beckham.
- He's a fashion icon, changing the style of his clothes, hair and accessories with bewildering frequency. (And what tattoos!)
- He's the doting father of three sons and a daughter.

The crazy gang

Goalkeepers are a breed apart. They may be more protected than before, but it takes a special courage to dive at the feet of a rampaging striker and dominate a penalty area as much by force of personality as by having a safe pair of hands. Here are three of the best:

• Lev Yashin
Known as the Black Spider, because he played in black and seemed to have eight arms, the Russian was the only keeper to win the European Footballer of the Year award (in 1963), and many feel he was the best of all time. He played in three World Cups from 1958, and his testimonial match drew a crowd of 100,000.

• Pat Jennings
The Northern Ireland no. 1 had an international career spanning 22 years, his last World Cup match falling on his 41st birthday – against Brazil in 1986. He had huge hands, but he also developed the technique (much used today) of saving with his feet.

• Dino Zoff
The International Federation of Football History and Statistics (IFFHS) voted the Italian as the third-greatest goalkeeper of the 20th century behind Yashin and Gordon Banks (page 160). He became the oldest ever winner of the World Cup when he captained Italy in the 1982 tournament at the age of 40.

He's also, of course, extremely rich, and it seems that he can do no wrong – or, at least, no wrong that does him any harm in the image stakes.

Even in footballing terms, he led a charmed life. In 2007, after eleven successful years with Manchester United and four more with Real Madrid, he moved (for another fortune) to LA Galaxy in California. Since he was now 32, surely this was a form of early retirement. But, no – within 18 months 'Becks' was sharing his talents between Galaxy and the great AC Milan in Serie A, and still showing enough stamina to be called up to play for England. In 2013 he signed for Paris Saint-Germain, where he became the first English player to win league titles in four countries, before retiring shortly after his 38th birthday.

STATS CARD

Most clean sheets by goalkeepers:

10 Peter Shilton (England) 1982–1990
10 Fabien Barthez (France) 1998–2006

2010

- **Host country:** South Africa.

- **Finalists:** Algeria, Argentina, Australia, Brazil, Cameroon, Chile, Denmark, England, France, Germany, Greece, Italy, Ivory Coast, Ghana, Honduras, Japan, Mexico, Netherlands, New Zealand, Nigeria, North Korea, Paraguay, Portugal, Serbia, Slovakia, Slovenia, South Africa, South Korea, Spain, Switzerland, United States, Uruguay.

- **What happened:** The tournament was staged in Africa for the very first time – and for the very first time the hosts were eliminated in the opening round of matches. The ear-shattering vuvuzelas blown by the home supporters annoyed many visiting fans, but Sepp Blatter gave them his official blessing.

  Spain, already European champions and regarded pre-tournament as the best team in the world, duly beat the Netherlands 1–0 in the final – so becoming the first European country to win the trophy outside their own continent.

- **Champions:** Spain.

- **What happened next:** Spain went on to win the European championship again in 2012.

THAT SAMBA RHYTHM

You couldn't choose more different hosts for the World Cups in 2010 (South Africa, its team a footballing minnow) and 2014 (Brazil, the biggest fish in the pond), but both tournaments shared an unashamedly exotic theme.

Those first finals to be staged on the African continent became a celebration of the 'rainbow nation', with ex-president Nelson Mandela gushing that 'I feel like a young man of fifteen.' The Brazilians in turn decided to hype their sex appeal, with the slogan 'All in One Rhythm'.

South Africa 2010:
Some thought the fans'
fanfare a tad unfair.

South African exuberance brought us the vuvuzelas, single-note plastic horns whose excruciating noise was likened to a herd of flatulent elephants. Calls for them to be banned (the Japan defender Tulio complained that he couldn't hear a team-mate two metres away) were dismissed by FIFA's 'Mr Big', Sepp Blatter, who said: 'There should be no attempts to Europeanise this World Cup'.

The Brazilians, naturally, chose a percussion instrument as their equivalent. The caxirola – a plastic shaker – was given official blessing but was, incongruously, banned inside the stadiums. No, it wasn't because of the noise, but (a) because they might be used as weapons and (b) because, it was alleged, advertising slogans might be written on them. (FIFA, after all, always has its own approved clients to protect.) Oh, potentially violent and rampantly commercial World Cup!

Meanwhile Coca-Cola's 'global 2014 World Cup anthem' was unveiled as 'The World is Ours' by singer David Correy and the Brazilian percussion group Monobloco – and we don't dare reproduce a word of it here.

Grumbles and grouches

This being the World Cup, there have been some lively controversies – *of course!* For a start there's the moral argument about whether a country should be spending vast amounts of money on new stadiums and other facilities when so many of its inhabitants are living in poverty.

Pre-2010, the South African journalist Christopher Merrett wrote that FIFA had hired his country 'as a theatre in which to stage a highly lucrative media event and depart with the profit'. The financial analysts Grant Thornton took a very different view, claiming that more than 400,000 new jobs would be created by the tournament, with the economy benefiting by more than £4.4 billion.

Pre-2014, the same debate has raged in Brazil, with the great striker and 1994 World Cup winner Romario condemning the human cost of holding the event in his country. He did his sums and reckoned that for the amount spent on the football fest Brazil could have built eight thousand schools. 'It's a lack of respect, a lack of scruples,' he said – adding bitingly that 'The real president of our country is FIFA.'

A few news stories ahead of the 2014 tournament:

- **There were mass riots throughout the country in June 2013, with a million people on the streets and police using tear gas and rubber pellets against them. A hike in bus fares provided the original spark, but World Cup spending was soon caught up in the protests – with fears for public safety a year later.**

The stadiums

Twelve cities were chosen as venues for the 2014 tournament, the shortest distance between any two of them being 250 miles. The cost of building six new stadiums and revamping six old ones was estimated at £550 million, but it was also essential to improve airports, because flying was the only realistic travel option for fans and teams alike.

The largest stadium is the Maracanã in Rio, which holds nearly 80,000 fans. The most exotic location? The Vivaldão at Manaus in the Amazon rainforest.

World Cup mascots

The 1966 World Cup in England began what has become a tradition of creating a cheeky mascot based on characteristics of the host nation:

1966 (England) World Cup Willie – a lion wearing an England shirt.

1970 (Mexico) Juanito – a boy wearing Mexico's kit and a sombrero.

1974 (West Germany) Tip and Tap – two boys wearing the national kit.

1978 (Argentina) Gauchito – a gaucho boy wearing a hat and neckerchief and carrying a whip.

1982 (Spain) Naranjito – An orange wearing the Spanish kit.

1986 (Mexico) Pique – a moustachioed jalapeño pepper wearing a sombrero.

1990 (Italy) Ciao – a stick figure with a football head and an Italian tricolour body.

1994 (United States) Striker the World Cup Pup – a dog wearing a red, white and blue football kit.

1998 (France) Footix (after Asterix) – a blue rooster.

2002 (South Korea and Japan) Ato, Kaz and Nik (the Speriks) – orange, purple and blue computer-generated creatures, their names selected from a shortlist suggested by Internet users and customers of McDonald's.

2006 (Germany) Goleo VI and Pille – a lion wearing a German shirt and his sidekick, a talking football.

2010 (South Africa) Zakumi – a yellow leopard with green hair.

2014 (Brazil) Fuleco – a three-banded armadillo, yellow with green shorts and a blue shell and tail.

- FIFA pressure obliged Brazil to suspend its ban on alcohol inside stadiums for the duration of the World Cup, despite its success in curbing violence – Budweiser being one of the event's major sponsors.

- The Brazilian tourist board warned that some hotels were hiking their prices by more than 500 per cent during the World Cup, with potential harm to long-term tourism in the country.

- After continual allegations of corruption against him, the president of Brazil's football confederation, Ricardo Teixeira, resigned 'for health reasons'. The former FA chairman Lord Triesman had accused Teixeira of offering him bribes to favour England's unsuccessful bid to stage the 2018 finals.

STATS CARD

Countries scoring most goals in one tournament before 2014:

Hungary (1954)	27
Germany FR (1954)	25
France (1958)	23
Brazil (1950)	22
Brazil (1970)	19

Eyes in the sky

It was Frank Lampard's disallowed goal for England against Germany in the 2010 finals that made the previously sceptical Sepp Blatter a convert to goal-line technology. England were battling back from being 2-0 down, and this would have been their equaliser. As the TV cameras clearly showed, Lampard's shot hit the bar and came down well over the line, but the officials ruled the effort out – and Germany went on to complete a comfortable 4-1 victory.

The contract to provide sophisticated spot-the-ball equipment for the 2014 finals was, ironically, won by the German-based GoalControl company. Their system involves the positioning of 14 high-speed cameras above and around the goals, not only capturing the position of the ball in three dimensions to within a few millimetres, but filtering players, match officials and any extraneous objects out of the picture and relaying the evidence to officials' watches in less than a second.

Alex Horne, the FA's general secretary, welcomed the move as 'one of the biggest changes that has happened in the 150 years since we conceived the laws of the game'.

And Lampard's verdict? 'It's a no-brainer,' he said.

2014: The groups

The group matches, on a league basis, begin on 12 June and continue until 26 June. The top two teams from each group advance to a series of knock-out rounds, with the Final being played on Sunday 13 July 2014.

Group A
Brazil, Croatia, Mexico, Cameroon

Group B
Spain, Netherlands, Chile, Australia

Group C
Colombia, Greece, Côte d'Ivoire, Japan

Group D
Uruguay, Costa Rica, England, Italy

Group E
Switzerland, Ecuador, France, Honduras

Group F
Argentina, Bosnia-Herzegovina, Iran, Nigeria

Group G
Germany, Portugal, Ghana, USA

Group H
Belgium, Algeria, Russia, Korea Republic

When the whistle blows

And yet, and yet… the fiercest critic knows that once the tournament is in motion the dirty deals, the misspent cash, the bitter backbiting and all the vainglorious over-the-top hype are temporarily put aside.

There were three exciting strikers the footballing world would be urging to perform at their scintillating best. In the yellow and green of Brazil, **Neymar** – the 22-year-old billed as the new Pelé. In the blue and white stripes of Argentina, **Lionel Messi** – the holder of umpteen goalscoring records and widely acclaimed the best player in the world. And in the red of Portugal, Messi's one major rival for the top-dog accolade, **Cristiano Ronaldo** – the free-scoring Real Madrid star whose country had endured a nail-biting series of matches even to qualify for the finals.

But football is full of surprises. Somewhere among the ranks of the relative unknowns there would be lurking a player just waiting to upstage the elite and claim a place for himself in World Cup history . . .

Glossary

Anschluss The incorporation of Austria into Germany by the Nazis.

apartheid A system of segregation on grounds of race, practised in South Africa from 1948 to 1984.

bye (as in **to be given a bye**) To move into the next round of a competition without having to play anyone, due to lack of opponents.

clean sheet Not conceding a goal in a football match.

dugout A manager's area by the side of the pitch.

feinting A move of the body to trick another player into believing you are going one way, when actually going the other.

lapis lazuli A bright blue semiprecious stone, used to make the pigment ultramarine.

linos A colloquial term for linesmen, the second and third officals in a match, who since 1996 have been renamed 'assistant referees'.

politburo Short for Politisches Büro des Zentralkomitees, a communist party's committee for deciding policy.

seeding The overall ranking of a team in world terms, used to organise tournaments such as the World Cup.

slush fund A sum of money set aside to be used for bribery.

World Cup Timeline

1863 English Football Association founded.
1904 FIFA founded, with Robert Guérin as president.
1906 English FA joins FIFA. Daniel Burley Woolfall becomes FIFA president.
1908 England are Olympic champion.
1912 England Olympic champions again.
1914–1918 First World War brings a halt to sporting events. UK football associations withdraw from FIFA over issue of playing against teams who have arranged fixtures with Germany.
1921 Jules Rimet becomes FIFA president.
1924 Uruguay are Olympic champions.
1928 English FA resigns from FIFA over 'broken time' payments. Uruguay are Olympic champions again. FIFA committee formed to organise the first World Cup.
1930 First World Cup held in Uruguay, won by the host country.
1934 World Cup in Italy, won by hosts. Mussolini provides his own cup.
1936 Berlin Olympics.
1938 Germany annexes Austria, which

withdraws from World Cup in France, won by Italy.

1939–1945 Second World War.

1946 England and the three other UK football associations rejoin FIFA.

1950 World Cup in Brazil, won by Uruguay.

1954 World Cup in Switzerland, won by West Germany.

1956 Uprising in Hungary put down by Soviet tanks. Several members of great Hungarian team leave to play in western Europe.

1958 South Africa is expelled from the African Cup of Nations because of its apartheid policy. World Cup in Sweden, won by Brazil.

1961 South Africa suspended by FIFA. Stanley Rous becomes FIFA president.

1962 World Cup in Chile, won by Brazil.

1963 South Africa's suspension lifted.

1964 South Africa's suspension reimposed.

1966 Jules Rimet Trophy stolen in London, and found by dog called Pickles. World Cup in England, won by hosts.

1969 The 'football war' between Honduras and El Salvador.

1970 World Cup in Mexico. Won by Brazil,

who keep the Jules Rimet Trophy.

1974 João Havelange becomes FIFA president. World Cup in West Germany, won by hosts.

1975 Soweto uprising brutally suppressed. South Africa expelled from FIFA.

1976 Military coup in Argentina. FIFA decides that 1978 World Cup should go ahead there.

1978 Attempted kidnap of France coach Michel Hidalgo in protest against Argentine regime. World Cup in Argentina, won by hosts.

1982 Falklands War. World Cup in Spain, won by Italy.

1983 Jules Rimet Trophy stolen from the Brazilian Federation of Football headquarters and never seen again.

1986 World Cup in Mexico, won by Argentina. Andrés Escobar, who scored an own goal in the finals, is shot dead after returning to Colombia.

1990 World Cup in Italy, won by West Germany.

1994 World Cup in USA, won by Brazil.

1998 Sepp Blatter becomes FIFA president. World Cup in France, won by hosts.

2002 Failed attempt to remove Sepp Blatter as FIFA president amid corruption charges. World Cup in Japan and South Korea, won by Brazil.
2006 World Cup in Germany, won by Italy.
2010 World Cup in South Africa, won by Spain.
2014 20th World Cup, in Brazil.

further reading

Among the sources used for this book were:

Complete Book of the World Cup
    Cris Freddi, HarperSport
The Soccer War
    Ryszard Kapuscinski, Granta Books
The Story of the World Cup
    Brian Glanville, Faber & Faber
World Cup Stories
    Chris Hunt, BBC

Index

STATS CARD INDEX

A handy reference guide to the scintillating stats found throughout the pages of this book:

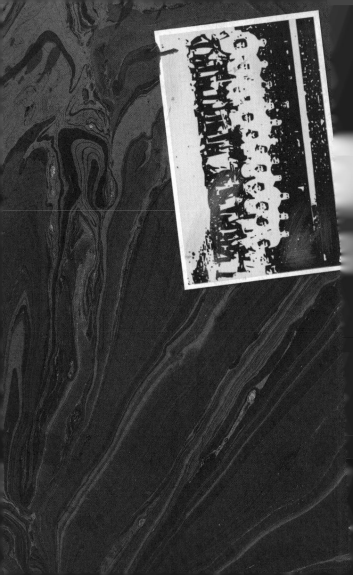